# HOW TO HEAL FROM EMOTIONALLY IMMATURE PARENTS

*Published in the United States by:*
Hay House LLC, www.hayhouse.com®
P.O. Box 5100, Carlsbad, CA, 92018-5100





The information given in this book should not be treated as a substitute for professional medical advice; always consult a medical practitioner. Any use of information in this book is at the reader's discretion and risk. Neither the author nor the publisher can be held responsible for any loss, claim or damage arising out of the use, or misuse, of the suggestions made, the failure to take medical advice or for any material on third-party websites.

Client names have been changed to maintain confidentiality.

A catalogue record for this book is available from the British Library.

Tradepaper ISBN: 978-1-4019-9857-8
E-book ISBN: 978-1-83782-471-7
Audiobook ISBN: 978-1-83782-469-4

1st Printing

Printed in the United States of America

This product uses responsibly sourced papers, including recycled materials and materials from other controlled sources.

The authorized representative in the EU for product safety and compliance is Penguin Random House Ireland, Morrison Chambers, 32 Nassau Street, Dublin D02 YH68, Ireland. https://eu-contact.penguin.ie

# HOW TO HEAL FROM EMOTIONALLY IMMATURE PARENTS

SIAN MORGAN-CROSSLEY

HAY HOUSE
Carlsbad, California • New York City
London • Sydney • New Delhi

*This book is for anyone who spent their childhood knocking on a door that their parents never opened.*

*Also for Aphra and Shay, my little loves.*
*I promise to keep learning and healing so*
*that I can be the parent you both deserve.*

# CONTENTS

# INTRODUCTION

I hadn't long qualified as a therapist when I found myself working with Janie. She came for sessions after being signed off from work with stress. In our first meeting, she talked about the three years of frequent 12-hour workdays that had led to her getting up from her desk and unceremoniously leaving the office in the middle of the day one Tuesday, and sobbing in a coffee shop for the rest of the afternoon, before going home and staying there until our session two weeks later. In that first meeting, she also spoke about her sadness at not having a partner, and the string of painful relationships she'd had in recent years that had left her feeling terrible about herself. Her friendships were difficult and she was on her fifth fad diet of the year in a bid to lose the weight that she saw as vital to be lost in order for her to have a good life. She felt defeated.

Ready to help her with my recently acquired knowledge of how childhood shapes us, and how the unconscious patterns we pick up from our relationship with our parents play out in our adult life, I was preparing to dive in and help her unearth the root causes behind what had been happening in her life lately.

However, as I invited Janie to talk about what life was like for her growing up, and inquired about her parents, I hit a wall. She said that she'd had a good childhood and listed the common markers: She lived in a nice house in a nice area, attended a good school, and left with good grades. She had two brothers, who she mostly got on with, and she went on family holidays at least once a year. She used the word 'normal' more times than I could count and told me in various ways that there was nothing to report; her parents weren't perfect but had done their best, and that was the end of that.

Fast-forward eight weeks and it transpired that Janie's mother was intensely competitive with her. She hated Janie getting attention from anyone – whether that was from her own family or from complete strangers. Her mother was also extremely critical of Janie's appearance and academic achievements and ultimately, no matter how hard she pushed herself, she could never quite do enough to please her mother. Her father was home at 5 p.m. on the dot each day, and he clocked out emotionally from Janie and her brothers at 5:01. She said he was always there, but never *really* there. To the outside world, he was a present, devoted father who worked hard for the family (which Janie said he absolutely did). But as a dad, he was ultimately disinterested.

Janie's original unwillingness to talk about her parents became a common thread with many of my clients. There are, of course, various different and individual reasons for this, but if I think back to how 20-year-old, pre-therapied me might have responded to the question, 'What was your childhood like?' or 'What were your parents like?' I imagine I might have put myself in the category of saying, 'It wasn't too bad,' or 'Other people had it so much worse.' I realize now that these common responses are built-in cultural mechanisms that help us to maintain a feeling that everything was OK and that we and our family are 'normal.' However, while their function is to protect us, these kinds of stock responses also stop us from applying critical thinking and really considering what life might have felt like for us during those precious, formative, early years of life.

Fast-forward 20 years and many therapy sessions later, however, and I would say that I had a childhood in which my practical needs were met, but my emotional needs were not. The impact of that on my life has been subtle but considerable. I've never veered too far in either direction off the scale of a socially acceptable life and have, from the outside, 'done OK.' I've ticked off many of those made-up metaphorical boxes as someone who is married, has two very lovely children, and a successful career; however, over the years I've also battled with eating disorders and bouts of anxiety and depression that made absolutely no sense when looking at my generally nice life. I lived my 20s as a very timid, fearful version of myself, have routinely felt not good enough, and have been not-too-interested in living at certain points over the years. As I sit here now, most of those struggles are largely behind me, but in order to get here I've had to get very honest about how my mother's control and dominance, my father's apathy for all things concerning family life, and their persistent arguments during my childhood years affected me. It took some time for me to realize that growing up in a nice house in a lovely part of the UK doesn't necessarily make for an emotionally healthy childhood.

So many of us are born into families with traumatized people running the show. Our parents lived their own story before having us and unfortunately many people still have a lot left to resolve when they become parents. This often means that innocent children are swept up in their parents' trauma narrative. Family life becomes the stage on which your parents' issues, regrets, suffering, and frustrations are played out. This is painful and emotionally damaging, and what makes it even more confusing is that you could have been having a miserable time as a child, while it seemed to the outside world that you had perfectly nice, reasonable, mature parents. But in truth, emotional maturity has nothing to do with age, or life circumstances. I wish more people knew that, in fact, having emotionally immature parents is like being parented by a 10-year-old with a mortgage.

## AGE IS MORE THAN A NUMBER

I often wonder who decided the age at which we officially become an adult. The age when we are (suddenly) deemed capable of getting married, driving a car, drinking alcohol, becoming parents, and owning a home. Overnight we move from adolescent to adult, and what's not accounted for is the fact that someone's *emotional age* can be very different to their birth age.

We each have an emotional age (which can vary in different areas of our life) and it has very little to do with how many years we've been alive, or how 'grown up' we seem. Emotional age relates to how able we are to cope with the emotional aspects of life: relationship issues, daily stressors, criticism, rejection, anxiety, disappointment, vulnerability, loss, anger, sadness. It also relates to our ability to self-reflect. It is entirely possible to be in your 50s, with a sensible job, nice house, and healthy pension waiting for you, and have the emotional age of a teenager. Equally, you could be relatively young in chronological age, but have a good understanding of your emotional world, a well-regulated nervous system, and an understanding of how to be authentic, have healthy relationships, and self-reflect, making you emotionally mature.

How emotionally mature or immature you are as an adult is largely the result of your childhood experiences. If someone generally receives 'good enough parenting' and is able to develop without the need to heavily suppress themselves or attend to someone else's needs and emotions during their childhood, they will likely develop the capacity to cope with their feelings and manage life in a generally healthy way as an adult. If, however, a child finds themselves having to manage a lot of stress at an early age, or constantly put other people before themselves, or feels rejected or unloved, they will be more likely to be emotionally immature as an adult. Their childhood experiences will make it difficult for them to cope with stress, process difficult emotions, or handle conflict in relationships.

Emotional immaturity tends to show up most obviously in how people parent their own children, simply because parenting is one of the few jobs in life that requires both practical *and* emotional skills. Putting the relentless snacks, car rides, and tidying aside, parenting is ultimately about providing emotional regulation and forming a relationship, both of which require a range of emotional skills – such as the ability to be open, honest, boundaried, reflective, and self-aware – in order to be done in a healthy way.

Without these skills, parents often struggle to form a positive and robust dynamic with their child, which impacts the child in various ways, such as how confident they are, how they see themselves, and how able they are to have healthy relationships as adults (and so the cycle continues). No one approaches the task of parenting as a blank slate, and your parents' childhood wounds, challenges, gaps, and traumas will have affected their emotional age and the way they parented you. If you didn't experience your parent(s) as reliable, safe, and dedicated to understanding you, you were robbed of what you deserved as a child. Without a reliable and close connection to your parents, the world quickly feels unsafe for a child.

Emotionally immature people bring their unresolved trauma with them into parenthood. Your parents may be or have been competent adults in many other areas of life, but you might still have been parented by someone who was emotionally young and underdeveloped. Someone who hadn't yet learned how to form healthy relationships, or cope with their emotions, or manage stress. None of this lessens the impact on you, and your parents' unresolved trauma doesn't excuse their behavior toward you, but it does give us a way to start making sense of it. Your childhood was an unconscious echo of what your parents experienced as children themselves. Their childhood was likely a slightly altered version of your grandparents' childhood, and so on and so forth. You are part of that cycle, but now it's time to step out of it and start creating a new and healthier cycle instead.

## YES, BUT HOW?

So how do you heal from a childhood with emotionally immature parents that has left you feeling deficient and emotionally disoriented? The following three stages are what I've found (personally and professionally) to be most effective when healing from emotionally immature parenting, and this book will take you along these three stepping stones so that you can come out the other side more aware of how your childhood has shaped you, less weighed down by your parents' unresolved trauma, and clearer about who you are and what you want from the rest of your life.

1. **Understanding:** Firstly, we'll get clear on how your childhood felt for you, and how you experienced your parents (no corroboration from siblings, parents, or other family members needed – this is about your experience). Then we'll work through the feelings of guilt that so often interfere with healing from emotionally immature parenting. This section will also be a crash course in learning about 'little t' trauma, and understanding some of the science behind how trauma affects the brain and body.

2. **Accepting and Grieving:** Once you have a solid understanding of how your mother, father, or both have affected you, it's time for the emotional but necessary part of accepting it and grieving what you didn't get. You'll be guided through the process of mourning the loss of the parental relationship that you needed as a child (and still need as an adult). This is about accepting what was and releasing what might have been. It may be useful to note that forgiveness doesn't come into this (unless you want to

work on that yourself, as a bonus step!). Acceptance and grief create space, increase capacity for deeper healing, and establish the foundation for the next stage.

3. **Healing:** In the final section, we'll start by focusing on the cornerstone of any emotionally healthy life: self-parenting. This is something emotionally healthy and independent people automatically do, but if you had emotionally immature parents, you'll probably need to learn how to parent yourself well. You'll learn how to tend to your nervous system, develop internal safety, and create a life that tends to your needs and well-being. You'll also learn the skills of self-compassion, healthy boundaries, self-discipline, and self-nurture. By this stage, you will hopefully feel lighter, clearer, and with more awareness and conscious intention than when you started this book. We began by looking at the past and will end with our eyes on the future. This is where you'll get clear on your values and use this to fuel a full life that's in alignment with who you are. This includes improving your relationships so that you can benefit from close, healthy connections, which we all need to thrive. You'll explore what a well-lived life means for *you* and start taking steps toward that.

Growing up with parents who are not emotionally aware turns childhood into a survival mission. I'm so sorry you had to go through that, and I'm honored and ready to be a small part of your process of reclaiming a sense of safety in the world and connection with yourself.

■ ■ ■ ■

Throughout the book, I refer to parent or parent(s) interchangeably, but everything that's discussed can be applied to your mother only, or your father only, or to both. It can also be applied to stepparents, grandparents, or anyone who was a central guiding parental figure when you were growing up. I have used the terms 'mother' and 'father' throughout the book, but this is not designed to alienate those who were raised with two mothers or two fathers. All the information in the book can be applied regardless of the gender of your parents. I'm also aware that you may come to this book at various stages of relationship with your parent(s) now. Whether you are in daily contact with them, have no contact at all, have lost them through death, have occasional contact, or something in between, this book can help you heal. The focus is on your childhood years, and by understanding, grieving, and processing how your parents related to you when you were developing, much can be shifted and improved in your life now. So, without further ado, let's get started by taking a look at the different *types* of emotionally immature parents.

# PART I
# UNDERSTANDING

CHAPTER 1

# WHAT IS EMOTIONALLY IMMATURE PARENTING?

I looked out the car window, nervously waiting to be told whether I'd passed the test or not. After three tries, I'd finally done it! I'd passed my driving test and felt like I was about to burst with excitement. I got home and ran inside to tell my parents. It was the proudest I'd been of myself during my 19 years, and I instantly asked if I could drive my mum round the block. I drove for 10 seconds, before she screamed at me to stop and got out of the car saying, 'I'm not going to be part of your first car crash, Sian.'

In that moment, I saw it clearly:

- Her instinct to protect herself was stronger than her desire to connect with me.
- Her personal anxieties carried more weight than her love for me.

- A lack of confidence in herself had become a lack of confidence in me (she didn't see me as my own person and therefore projected her own self-doubt onto me).

This is one of many stories that spring to mind in which my parents' needs, anxieties, past traumas, and projections got in the way of them being able to see me and connect with me as a child. I have no doubt you have many moments from your own childhood (that may come to mind or may simply be stored unconsciously) that left you feeling the unbalancing effects of emotionally immature parenting. Moments that made your childhood more confusing and difficult than it should have been. Moments that led you to reading this book.

It's time to start making more sense of those moments so that they become less significant. As you read this book, it's my hope that the moments in which your parents' emotional immaturity negatively affected you lose their power, and that they become a small part of your story, rather than a main part of the plot. I hope that you get some distance from your childhood, so that it doesn't affect your life now so much. One of the ways we will ultimately find this distance is by getting closer to your childhood, so that you can process it and consciously move away. Let's start by getting clear on what emotionally immature parenting actually looks like. There isn't one single trait that makes a parent emotionally immature, but below are the 10 most common *types* of emotionally immature parent. You might strongly recognize one or two, or find familiarity in them all. I hope these summaries will help you to get to know more about your parents, yourself, and your childhood.

## THE 10 TYPES OF EMOTIONALLY IMMATURE PARENT

### 1. The 'Do It My Way' Parent

This was very nearly the 'I know what's best for you' parent. This parent tends to live with the belief that there is a 'right' and 'wrong' way to do and be and live. They typically live by these rules themselves because it feels safest for them and gives them the illusion of control (and they often confuse control with security). The point at which it becomes emotionally immature parenting is when they attempt to enforce these rigid rules on their children, often long into adulthood. They will likely use emotions like disappointment, shame, and anger to try to put their children off making 'wrong' decisions and to steer them toward their definition of a well-lived life. This undermines the capacity of their child to live their life in the way they want to as an adult. A healthy parent-child relationship requires a bit of flexibility and an understanding that the child is an autonomous, separate person, which this parent doesn't fully grasp.

#### *What's Underneath It All?*

At the core, this is a person who finds it very difficult to not be in control and who fears being abandoned. Trying to exert control (over themselves and other people) and keep their children close is their way of managing their anxiety. This likely stems from either not having enough autonomy themselves as a child and teenager, or having too much responsibility too soon, meaning they didn't have enough protection from the adults around them as a child, creating deep-rooted anxiety. This type of parent needs their worldview reinforced. They crave reassurance that the way they have chosen to live is correct and they do this by making it the only option and trying to eliminate their children's attempts to do things differently. When their toddler, teenager, or adult child chooses to do something that sits outside of their parameters of what is right and what is wrong, it feels like a personal attack on how they have chosen to live their lives.

## 2. The 'On the Defense' Parent

This is a highly reactive parenting dynamic in which, as their child, you can easily say or do the wrong thing and end up in a confusing argument, having to defend yourself, which becomes a common and tiring cycle. These parents are quick to misinterpret communication (from those close to them) as a threat or criticism, which makes them reactive and defensive. The 'on the defense' parent feels easily criticized and doesn't take feedback of any kind very well. You would likely have had to walk around on eggshells to avoid them blowing up, and may have become good at reading people's moods and facial expressions as a way of managing the relationship with your parent. The unpredictability of this dynamic can mean your childhood was lived in a fight-or-flight state, as you had to stay on high alert most of the time. It is very unlikely that they would ever have apologized to you, even when you absolutely deserved an apology.

Play, fun, and silliness aren't really part of the deal here. It's unlikely the 'on the defense' parent would have been able to spend much time relaxing with you or having fun, making it hard to bond with one another.

### *What's Underneath It All?*

This is parenting in fight-or-flight mode, the result of a dysregulated nervous system that is constantly scanning for threat and viewing relationships (including those with their children) through the lens of attack and defense. This is likely a trauma response to their own childhood or past experiences – experiences that left them feeling emotionally unsafe around people and particularly sensitive to criticism. Their childhood likely led them to believe that people can hurt them and that they need to preempt this and keep people (including their children) at a distance.

## 3. The 'Be on My Side Please' Parent

Having a child who agrees and never challenges them is what this parent requires to be OK. There is a tendency for this type of emotionally immature parent to slip into victimhood or martyrdom. You probably had the sense that they would get upset easily and were too sensitive to take the weight of you and your needs and boundaries. Their need to be constantly supported and never challenged makes it difficult to be yourself in this relationship. This type of parent can be triggered by something as simple as you disagreeing with them, which will hurt them and precipitate their disapproval, withdrawal, or sadness, making it impossible to set boundaries for fear of upsetting them. However, it might also have been seen when your parents were arguing with each other and the 'be on my side please' parent inappropriately tried to enlist your support. It's easy to feel sorry for the 'be on my side please' parent and it can be hard to acknowledge and prioritize your own feelings because you would have become used to protecting their feelings, making it a particularly tricky dynamic to heal from.

### *What's Underneath It All?*

This is codependency 101, stemming from a lack of a sense of self which leaves a gap that this person looks to other people to fill. (*For more on codependency, see pages 166–168.*) The 'be on my side please' parent has learned to sacrifice their own needs and boundaries for other people, and they expect the same in return. They have a fear of abandonment and a deep need to be understood, accepted, and unconditionally loved by everyone (though this is really what a child needs from their parent, rather than the other way around). This is likely because they didn't get enough unconditional love and acceptance from their own parents, meaning that these needs have persisted in an intense way into adulthood. They may have consciously or unconsciously viewed having a child as a way to ensure they have an ally and constant form of support.

## 4. The 'Parenting Is Such an Inconvenience' Parent

Parenting *is* hard work. It requires a lot of your energy and resources and is full of practical and emotional challenges, which it is perfectly healthy to acknowledge. However, this type of emotionally immature parent makes this their focus and makes sure that their child knows that parenting them is hard work. Their belief that being a parent is getting in the way of their life can lead to various dynamics including:

- being resentful of their child

- expecting their child to be endlessly grateful to them
- being dismissive of their child's feelings as they stay consumed with their own

This type of parent focuses on how difficult it is to be a parent, while overlooking how difficult it feels to be their child! You would likely have been made to feel like you are difficult, in the way, and hard work, and there would have been a clear or subtle expectation for you to be grateful and to make your parents' life easier as much as you could. There is often a sense that the parent is a martyr in this dynamic, feeling hard done by and in a permanent state of struggle.

### *What's Underneath It All?*

Focusing on the difficult parts of their life has become automatic for this type of parent and they likely have low stress tolerance after experiencing too much stress early in life, or for long periods of time. They may live life in the position of a victim, and may well have been a victim of abuse or trauma as a child. As a result, they have developed an identity related to hardship, struggle, and adversity. They are constantly dissatisfied and often pull the people around them into that feeling of dissatisfaction. The 'parenting is such an inconvenience' parent can also result from a lack of support and access to the resources (time, money, education) and opportunities that they need. This style of parenting can also be triggered by them not having had the chance to live their pre-parenting life the way they wanted to, perhaps due to having to cope with their own family dysfunction, becoming a parent at a young age, or spending time grieving, dealing with trauma, or experiencing illness.

## 5. The 'Everything's Fine' Parent

This is a parent who can't cope with or understand difficult emotions (such as anger, sadness, and anxiety) in themselves or their children. They tend to minimize, ignore, or dismiss problems and issues that their children might have. Their unconscious desire is to have a home that is full of positive or neutral emotions only, and this can lead to pockets of denial and a lack of emotional expression and authenticity in the parent-child relationship. It can also be invalidating, especially when their child has complex feelings to sort through and the parent minimizes their experience.

Common phrases of the 'everything's fine' parent:

- 'Let's just calm down.'
- 'You're being very dramatic.'
- 'I'm so glad I never have to worry about you.'
- 'You're fine.'
- 'Stop making a fuss.'
- 'You're making a big deal of this; you'll be fine.'

You may have been praised for being 'fine.' There is often a lack of action or response if their child is struggling emotionally, and they will usually take the 'let's wait and see' approach (mainly because they don't know what else to do). This parenting dynamic would have been frustrating for you as their child because there would have been chunks of your life and experience that were denied, avoided, or not acknowledged. It can also make it difficult for you to cope with your full range of feelings as an adult, because you wouldn't have had guidance or modeling for how to cope with feelings like anger, jealousy, rage, sadness, or anxiety.

### *What's Underneath It All?*

This approach is usually the result of a parent who didn't get much emotional input during their childhood, meaning they lack emotional awareness and understanding, and don't have a vocabulary for their feelings. They are emotionally avoidant as a result and have learned to suppress their own feelings, such as anger or sadness, from a young age. Therefore, they find it difficult to help their children with their feelings without being triggered. They likely have a low stress tolerance and typically avoid challenging situations, which makes it all the more difficult for them to help their children with their problems, or to face their difficult emotions.

## 6. The 'Not That Interested' Parent

There is generally a lack of warmth and affection here. A disinterest in the details of your life combined with a lack of time spent together makes it difficult to feel close to the 'not that interested' parent. This was very nearly named the 'emotionally unavailable parent' because parents who aren't really interested in their children in any real, substantial way tend also to be unavailable for emotional connection. This parent may have been preoccupied with their career or social life, to the exclusion of time with you. Your emotions would probably have been treated like an inconvenience, and emotional outbursts of any kind would have been frowned upon (or ignored). This type of emotionally immature parent is one of the most damaging when it comes to self-esteem because they can't really 'see' their children. They are unable to really know or understand their children, and they wouldn't have been able to witness your inner world, potential, and innate value. This often creates the tendency to feel not good enough or worth getting to know. You may have tried to get their attention in various ways; either through excelling and becoming an over-achiever, or through 'bad' behavior that you knew would catch their attention and create some contact with them. You might also find that you've unconsciously re-created the dynamic in some of your adult relationships, finding your way to people who aren't emotionally available or who don't easily give their attention or affection. This makes sense as a way of creating familiar dynamics and attempting to create a different outcome to the one you experienced with your 'not that interested' parent.

### *What's Underneath It All?*

This is a parent who probably didn't get enough love from their own parents when they were young, meaning they grew up not valuing authentic human connection. They are likely to be emotionally detached, numb, and avoidant, meaning they are less interested in relationships in general and more focused on things, achievements, and the material aspects of life. There can also be an element of depression underpinning the disinterest in their children. This is often so long-standing that it seems like part of their personality and therefore sadly remains untreated.

## 7. The 'Bully' Parent

This type of emotionally immature parent thinks they are entitled to respect from their child simply because they're their parent. There is often an obsession with getting the child to comply and obey them, and to do whatever they ask without protest. The 'bully' parent often makes their child feel small, insignificant, or stupid. The range of behaviors can be quite broad here; from low level but persistent teasing, to aggressive intimidation and violence. This type of parent will often make comments to or about their child in front of other people that are designed to humiliate them. They are likely inherently triggered by their child and, more specifically, the parts of their child that remind them of themselves, which they have not yet learned to accept. This parenting dynamic is very painful and undermining, and can create the experience of being victimized (which can stay with you as you leave childhood).

### *What's Underneath It All?*

The 'bully' parent was exposed to a lot of criticism and aggressive parenting themselves as a child, perhaps experiencing violence from their parent. There is often a feeling of inferiority underpinning this style of parenting, with the parent using their authority in their relationship with their child to feel in control, powerful, and dominant to mask feelings of being incompetent and ineffective in their life or relationships. A lot of this dynamic is often informed by the parent's anger toward themselves, which gets projected onto their children.

## 8. The 'Showing Their Feelings Without Dealing with Their Feelings' Parent

This type of parent tends to dominate the family home with their moods. This can be either with big, explosive reactions that feel disproportionate, or passive, moody comments that disrupt the balance and energy in the family. They can also be emotionally clumsy and unaware of the impact they're having. Their barbed comments affect everyone, without anyone being able to respond or question or make sense of them because they aren't delivered directly; this is passive-aggressive behavior at its finest. As their child, you may identify now as an empath or highly sensitive person because you had to learn how to read moods and emotions as clear explanations weren't offered. You may have learned to walk on eggshells to avoid triggering their explosions, and you may find it difficult to cope with your own emotions now, without having a model of what healthy emotional processing looks like.

### *What's Underneath It All?*

This type of emotionally immature parent craves being seen and understood, while also lacking emotional insight and the skills to communicate their feelings. They are unlikely to have had much emotional guidance from their own parents, leaving them lacking a language to express themselves. They likely never developed the skills to cope with their feelings in a healthy way, meaning their emotions stay hidden for periods of time and then spill out without much explanation.

## 9. The 'I Need to Be Needed' Parent

This dynamic can give the illusion of being a close parent-child relationship, but when you zoom in it's the parent's needs at the center of the relationship. This type of parent is often very helpful and reliable, and can bring many great things to the table, but it becomes emotionally immature parenting when their need to be needed and involved in their child's life becomes disabling for their child. The natural trajectory is for a developing person to become somewhat separate from their parents (which can be done while maintaining the relationship, when it's healthy), which creates space for their sense of self to develop and their independence to form. However, this is threatening to the 'I need to be needed' parent. As you strive to be more independent it might trigger your parent to unconsciously ask you to remain dependent and reliant on them when making decisions, functioning day to day, and knowing what you think and feel. You may keep yourself small, dependent, and reliant in some way in order to protect them.

### *What's Underneath It All?*

This parent's lack of identity and sense of self before having children means they have attached very strongly to the role of being a mother or father, and have used that to fill the internal void they felt before having children. They may also believe that their self-worth is reliant on them being helpful, useful, and caring, and are parenting from a place of low self-esteem. This can be the result of internalized patriarchy for mothers in particular. It can also simply be the way their low self-worth has manifested – as a desperation for their children to need them in order to remain in each other's lives. Their codependency makes the thought of their children being independent feel scary, stemming from their core fear of being alone.

## 10. The 'You're Not Good Enough' Parent

'You're too sensitive.'

'You're doing it wrong.'

'You could do with losing a few pounds.'

'Just try a bit harder next time.'

A constant stream of judgments, comparisons, and criticisms leaves the child of 'you're not good enough' parents feeling like they are constantly being assessed. The comments can be personal (how the child looks, their personality, their flaws) or more external (their achievements and decisions), but either way, the message is, 'You are not quite good enough as you are.' In this dynamic love is earned, and compassion and sympathy are nonexistent. The child's worth is tied directly to what they *do* rather than who they *are*, making it difficult for them to accept themselves or feel contented as an adult.

### *What's Underneath It All?*

The parent's feeling of being inadequate – which is often caused by them not getting unconditional love themselves as a child and needing to earn their parents' acceptance – underpins this type of emotional immaturity. Their harsh and superficial assessment of themselves has become their view of the world and informs how they see people (based on their appearance, achievements, and status). They unconsciously feel that they are not enough as they are and that they need to earn their place in the world, and they assume the same goes for their children, triggering this dynamic of judgment, criticism, and disapproval.

## THE CORE OF EMOTIONALLY IMMATURE PARENTING

Emotionally immature parents haven't developed the skills to handle their emotions or have healthy relationships. This creates a ripple effect that's felt most intensely by their children, because both of these skills are a core requirement for them if they are to grow into emotionally healthy adults. Although it has so many rewarding moments, emotionally mature parenting is ultimately a very selfless task. The focus needs to be, for the most part, on the child and their needs. This isn't to say that parents suddenly no longer have their own sense of self or their own needs – but an emotionally mature parent knows that their child is experiencing the world with an undeveloped brain, and that they therefore need more focus, attention, patience, and input in order to thrive and ultimately develop a brain of their own that will serve them well for the rest of their life. However, not all parents go into child-rearing with this awareness. Many become parents because they think they should, and their reflection on why they are becoming parents, and what that role involves, ends there. Others become parents because they believe (unconsciously) that having children might be a way to make life better or might make them feel like a more valid person.

And so a parent-child dynamic that's based on what the child can do for the parent, rather than the other way around, is born. The parent may take care of the child's practical needs, but the adult's emotional needs are at the center. Emotionally immature parents often use their children to fill emotional deficits from their childhood and voids in their own life. Voids like feeling lonely, unloved, out of control, or ineffective. We can see from the 10 types of parent described above that emotional immaturity can show up in various ways, but there are some common threads:

- The parent's emotional needs are front and center of the relationship.
- The parent is unable to meet your emotional needs or is overwhelmed by your emotions.
- You have to parent them in some way.
- They can't hear what you say or validate how you feel.
- The parent's boundaries are either too loose (they overshare or intrude in your life) or too rigid (they are very strict and uncompromising). Or a mixture of the two.

## WHAT IS EMOTIONALLY MATURE PARENTING?

As with emotionally immature parenting, there's no one way to be an emotionally mature parent. There are a million nuanced and individual ways in which parents who are generally emotionally aware might be with their children. There are some basic common themes though. An emotionally mature parent generally:

- takes responsibility for themselves, their problems, and their feelings, and **doesn't blame their children** or other people for their issues
- parents with an awareness of how emotions work and **how their children might be feeling**, rather than just focusing on how they are behaving
- recognizes their child as **a separate, autonomous individual** with their own wants, needs, and sense of self
- actively works on resolving their own trauma and is **committed to trying to stay as mentally healthy** as they can
- **doesn't depend** on their child for comfort, companionship, reassurance, or validation
- **apologizes** when they are in the wrong

All of this comes with the caveat that emotionally mature parents show up in this way *most* of the time. Not all the time. Emotionally mature parenting does not mean perfect parenting. It includes mistakes (and apologies). It involves being human and having fluctuating moods, bad days, and a range of emotions. It means accepting accountability for your issues, blocks, and personal pain and trying to do what you can to heal. Emotionally mature parenting is often imperfectly messy, but healthy and sturdy nonetheless. We will return to this subject again, in Chapter 10, where we look at parenting in the context of your other relationships.

One of the ways emotionally immature parents defend themselves when their child or adult child expresses negative feelings about them is by suggesting that the child is being too harsh or has expectations of them that are too high or unrealistic. However, it's been shown that parents do not need to provide a perfect relationship or environment for their children. In fact, all children need is for their parents to be 'good enough,' a term coined by pediatrician and psychoanalyst Donald Winnicott in the 1950s. He studied the parent-child relationship and noted that children don't need parents who are attuned and present and aware of their children's needs all the time. There is a lot of scope for parenting mistakes, and for challenges and ruptures in the parent-child relationship. Children are typically very forgiving of their parents.[1]

The fact that you actively need to recover from your relationship with your parent means that, at least at times, the parenting you received fell outside of these normal parameters. It indicates that you didn't get enough of what you needed, and that it was not 'good enough' parenting. Either the mistakes they made were too damaging (moments, events, or conversations that left you feeling deeply unsafe) or perhaps they were simply too frequent for you to move past unscathed. There are many ways in which parents can fall short of perfect parenting while staying within the remit of normal parenting. However, there are also many ways in which parents can do or say things that are impossible for a child to understand or recover from, and it's *those* experiences that create childhood wounds.

Let's take a moment to pull together what we've covered in this chapter by doing the exercise below. Write down your answers if you can, whether in a fancy new notebook dedicated to your healing or in 'Notes' on your phone (my personal favorite and most overused app). There will be various exercises to do throughout the book, and writing your responses will make the exercises more effective and impactful for you.

## MOVING FORWARD

Here's a reminder of the 10 types of emotionally immature parent to help you with this exercise:

1. The 'do it my way' parent
2. The 'on the defense' parent
3. The 'be on my side please' parent
4. The 'parenting is such an inconvenience' parent
5. The 'everything's fine' parent
6. The 'not that interested' parent
7. The 'bully' parent
8. The 'showing their feelings without dealing with their feelings' parent
9. The 'I need to be needed' parent
10. The 'you're not good enough' parent

Take some time to reflect on the following questions, and note down your answers:

- Which of the parenting types do you recognize most in your mother?

- Which of the parenting types do you recognize most in your father?
- Write down 3–5 new things that occurred to you about your parents or your childhood while reading this chapter.

Next, we're going to tackle that feeling that tends to plague those of us whose childhood looked fine but felt awful. If you have (occasional or frequent) moments when you feel guilty for questioning or criticizing your parents, because they gave you a roof over your head and food on the table, or if you question whether it was really that bad, or whether you're being oversensitive and making a fuss, the next chapter will help you get past this healing block so that you can take the actions that will improve your life and the lives of all those who come into contact with your new future self.

CHAPTER 2

# YOU'RE NOT MAKING A FUSS

Accurately assessing whether your childhood was bad enough to merit you being upset about it is, to use a phrase coined by philosopher Alan Watts, like trying to bite your own teeth. It's extremely difficult to do, and using other people's ideas and opinions to figure out whether your feelings about your own childhood are valid or not usually leads to an ongoing swirl of self-doubt, anger, and helplessness. There's always someone else's story to compare yours to; someone else who 'had it worse'; an ongoing weighing up of whether it was really that bad, or whether you are, in fact, making a fuss about nothing. But, with so many different opinions on what makes for a 'good' or 'bad' childhood, it's also difficult to trust *yourself* about how your childhood was.

Memory is complicated and unreliable, and it can be hard to recall exactly how life was for you growing up. The range of definitions of childhood trauma also make it confusing, and then there's the subtle societal pressure for people to be grateful to their parents no matter what, with frequent reminders that 'they did their best.' All of this makes it almost impossible to determine whether your relationship with your parents was (or is) problematic enough to warrant deeper reflection and consideration. Were they really that bad? Are my standards too high? Was I expecting too much? Am I being unfair?

It can be worth taking a step back and moving this from a cognitive process to an emotional one. This really isn't about objective facts or other people's opinions. If you feel that your parents didn't give you enough of what you needed, then it is so. If you know that life is harder for you now because of your childhood, then trust that. None of this is about what did or didn't happen; this is about how emotionally safe you felt with your parents, and how able you were to be yourself as a child. Your feelings about that are not up for debate. Luckily, it's also not a requirement for anyone else to agree with your version of events, or approve of how you feel about your childhood, in order for you to heal.

The idea that most other people have had the good fortune to have emotionally aware, attuned, psychologically healthy parents is just not true. Veena Kumari, Professor of Psychology at Brunel University, writes, 'Despite difficulties in recognizing and measuring emotional abuse, meta-analyses of the global prevalence of maltreatment convincingly reveal that childhood emotional abuse is self-reported by... about 36 percent [of the adult population].'[1] So, around one-third of the population recognizes that they didn't get what they needed emotionally from their parents or had adverse emotional experiences in childhood. Yet the notion that difficult childhoods are the fate of the unfortunate few persists.

## BUT THEY DID THEIR BEST

The idea that parents 'did their best' is at the core of many people's denial of the reality of their childhood experiences. For some, the suggestion that their parents did their best seems impossible in light of the things their parents did or didn't do during their childhood. For others, however, it's an idea that they hold on to tightly and use repeatedly to defend their parents (often to themselves). I'm actually not too interested in whether or not a parent did their best.

I suspect that most parents absolutely *do* do their best, some don't, and some sit somewhere in the middle. Whether a parent did their best or not is, unfortunately, largely irrelevant in terms of the impact their actions had on their child. A parent could have done their absolute best in the context of their own upbringing, mental or physical health issues, or economic circumstances, but this doesn't mean that their child got everything that they needed from them. A parent's best efforts can still result in parenting that is emotionally deficient.

I am certain that I am doing *my* best as a mother, *and* I strongly suspect my children will have gaps to fill when they are adults. The impact of my emotional blind spots, relational challenges, and the ways in which my unconscious childhood patterns show in my parenting will affect them, regardless of the work I do and continue to do on myself. Me trying my best doesn't automatically eradicate or fill these gaps. Good parental intention doesn't remove the need for healing.

## 'IT COULD'VE BEEN WORSE...'

Comparison is more than the thief of joy. It is also the thief of healing, recovery, and resolution after emotionally immature parenting. There will always be ways of invalidating your own experience by looking at someone else's and telling yourself that they had a worse time. It is, in some ways, a form of self-protection: re-categorizing your own experience so that it doesn't seem too bad. The issue with this, though, is that *childhood experiences are not relative*. The ways in which you were affected by a difficult interaction with your father when you were eight years old are unchanged by someone else's relatively 'worse' interaction with their father at eight years old.

Of course, childhood experiences do come in different forms and severity and it's not my intention to diminish the very serious incidents that some children endure. But as far as your nervous system is concerned, if you repeatedly experienced arguing parents, or feeling rejected, or feeling overpowered or helpless as a child, that would have been enough to put you into a fight-or-flight state, when you should have been feeling secure and carefree. (*For more on this, see Chapter 9.*) Minimizing the difficult parts of your childhood and your dynamic with your parents is often a symptom of not knowing how to take your feelings seriously (and sometimes the effect of frequently being told that you are dramatic or oversensitive or ungrateful as a child). However, the truth remains that the difficult parts of your dynamic with your parents existed and continue to exist in how you feel about yourself, how you connect with other people, and the decisions you make – and this is the case regardless of anyone else's childhood experiences.

It's also important to say that while no one has a perfect childhood, living with an emotionally immature parent is a special kind of unfairness that not everyone experiences. You deserved parents who gave you unconditional love, acceptance, and connection, not parents who were self-centered, insensitive, unkind, or emotionally unavailable. Regardless of the many ways this might have been dismissed (by yourself and others) over the years, please know that it was not OK and that you deserved much better.

## THE HORROR OF BEING UNGRATEFUL

Another common factor that sabotages the healing process and prolongs personal suffering is the internal battle of ingratitude and guilt. There is a narrative that is particularly strong among emotionally immature parents that children are indebted to them. In some cases, it goes as far as suggesting that children owe their parents for simply being alive, making that child's existence an exercise in repaying this debt to their parent with compliance and unwavering loyalty. Or you may have grown up with the more subtle, but still powerful, message that you as the child must be grateful to your parents no matter what: an expectation of unconditional gratitude without having experienced unconditional love.

You may, however, also find yourself caught up in a tussle of genuinely feeling grateful for many of the things your parents provided for you, and for the beneficial parts of your relationship with them and the role they've played in your life... while knowing that you have also suffered mentally and emotionally because of them. This is a difficult state to be in. Grateful and angry. Appreciative and exasperated. Genuinely recognizing the good and all that was done for you, and living with the daily evidence of the bad. It can be agonizing holding all of these opposing thoughts and feelings. There will undoubtedly be moments when your mind offers a more compelling argument for the case of being grateful to your parents, quickly followed by a sense of loyalty to your younger self and all they endured. Perhaps both things are true. Maybe they gave you things to be grateful for and they made mistakes that have been costly for you. Maybe you can hold both and honor both, and know that both are true for you. I've faced this tussle myself, and after wading through the layers of guilt, loyalty, and obligation, I've learned to feel genuine gratitude for all that my parents did for me – and the ways they sacrificed themselves to raise me — while still holding them accountable for the emotional and mental harm they caused. Gratitude doesn't cancel out accountability.

I grew up in a half-immigrant family, and the sacrifices made by my grandparents were significant. They moved from the warmth of the Caribbean to the cold, unwelcoming island of Great Britain in the 1960s, without the security of their ever-present family village around them, all in a bid to create a better life for their children and grandchildren. How unbearably difficult it must have been for them at times. My grandmother spoke often about her carefree childhood in Trinidad, picking mangoes from their garden, and her and her numerous cousins playing outside happily for hours. It seemed such a contrast to the struggles of starting a new life in England, my grandmother having to find work in factories having never worked previously, and the pain of not having enough money to fly back for her mother's funeral. They built a life here, but as with so many other immigrants throughout history, it came with enormous sacrifice for the whole family (including my mother, whose childhood was greatly affected by it all).

As with many children of immigrant families, I felt the weight of responsibility to make their hardship worthwhile. The message that I should be grateful to my parents and grandparents was ever-present when I was growing up. This is understandable in many ways; however, the issue with taking the position of being endlessly grateful to someone else is that it creates an enormous amount of pressure and guilt. Your life is then not really your own, you feel restricted and unable to reach your potential and live life fully, and so the sacrifices made by previous generations become somewhat pointless, in a sense. Surely what would make my ancestors' sacrifices worthwhile is me living a full, authentic, and good life in ways that they weren't able to? Feeling perpetually indebted and guilty doesn't allow for this.

Guilt is powerful, though, and it has the potential to derail even the most focused of healing journeys. While writing this book I conducted a survey with my online community, and 267 participants who identified as having had emotionally immature parents answered this question: 'Has feeling guilty affected you healing from emotionally immature parenting?' Here are some of the responses:

- 'I feel sorry for my parents constantly. The guilt was even stronger while growing up. It makes me feel bad to think about myself in it all.'
- 'I find myself feeling sorry for her at times, then other times she disgusts me, then she makes me frustrated, then guilty for feeling all of these feelings for a sole parent. When I think about how she hurt me it brings up all of those feelings and I become overwhelmed.'
- 'I feel sad for both my parents because of their limitations. I know I need to work on my own childhood stuff, but I feel so bad for them still.'
- 'I feel very sorry for my mum often. She spends a lot of energy trying to control our responses to her also, but I can't move past feeling sorry for her a lot of the time. It definitely stops me moving on.'

There comes a point in most childhood healing journeys at which you must, to some extent, choose between loyalty to your family and your personal emotional health. Unfortunately, it's rare that parents who were emotionally immature when their children were young do sufficient work on themselves for them to be aware, open, apologetic, and emotionally healthy by the time you are working through *your* childhood wounds. Sometimes, staying completely loyal to the family system you grew up in, and all the expectations and rules that come with that, means that you won't be able to heal fully. Old, entrenched family systems and dynamics are powerful and might not align with what you want for yourself now and in the future. This doesn't mean you can't have a relationship with your parents or your family, and it also doesn't mean you are actively betraying them. However, in order for you to live the rest of your life in a more emotionally healthy, conscious, and intentional state, you may have to decide to choose yourself. To choose to prioritize your own growth over continuing to be the daughter your mother expects you to be. To choose to acknowledge your feelings about your childhood rather than stick to the version of events that your father is happy with. Choosing yourself is likely to feel uncomfortable after years of preserving your loyalty to your family, but discomfort is a necessary part of growth, so it may be time to embrace it.

## THE SELF-TRUST BLOCK

When you are in a conversation with someone who is emotionally immature, it's not uncommon to feel like you're going a bit crazy. Suddenly the things you know to be true about the world are turned upside down. The rules for living that you've created, which help keep you grounded, can be blown open by an odd statement or baffling response. Sometimes interactions with emotionally immature people can feel anything from completely unreasonable, to strange, to comical, to utterly bizarre. It's common for you to be left doubting or deeply questioning yourself. Experiencing this as a child rocks the foundations of your ability to trust yourself, because you are being exposed to conversations and interactions that don't make sense. What's more, they are coming not only from an adult, but your parent, who you are primed to trust and follow and pay attention to. So you are faced with acknowledging that your parent is somewhat detached from reality (which is pretty damn scary for a child) – or you have to question yourself and wonder if *you* are the one who is detached from reality.

I remember as a child leaving many arguments with my mother completely bewildered, after trying to cope with her version of reality (and her attempts to obliterate mine). I had to listen to her pretend that she didn't say something that she had screamed five minutes earlier or claim that something she said meant something entirely different to what I thought it meant, and try to make sense of her version of events. This is one of the ways emotionally immature parents overwrite the innate and natural self-trust we are born with. In order to heal you must be able to trust yourself. You must trust that part of you that says your childhood was difficult in many ways, and that your parents have left marks that need to be tended to.

Self-trust can also be undermined by a parent who loved you, but didn't 'like' you. A parent who loved you in an obligatory, protective, biological sort of way, but who didn't *actually* like who you are as a person. Confusingly, this type of parent provides nurture and rejection simultaneously. If you grew up with a parent who did a great deal for you but rarely wanted to spend time with you, it can be hard to trust your instincts about the rejection you felt when there's also clear evidence that they cared. Knowing that your parent sacrificed so much to raise you – while also feeling that they judge you and your choices harshly – is deeply confusing. Being aware that your mother or father did the hard work of parenting, yet continually wished you were someone else, undermines self-trust because the message is incongruent and impossible to reconcile. As you heal, remember that it was only ever their lack of awareness and inability to examine their own triggers that allowed this uneasy dynamic of love and dislike to coexist.

Emotionally immature parenting typically damages self-trust because:

- The parents' needs are always front and center, forcing the child to ignore, suppress, or doubt their feelings in order to make space for their parent.
- There is often a lack of interest in the child's emotions and inner world, making it difficult for them to understand or trust what they feel.
- Emotionally immature parents can suck their children into their inner turmoil and extreme emotions, shaming and blaming them. This distorts the child's perception and makes it hard for them to trust themselves or their version of reality.
- Boundaries and instinct go hand in hand. If a parent doesn't acknowledge their child's boundaries, it makes the child doubt their instincts (*see pages 105–107*).

Trusting your feelings and knowing that your childhood was damaging can be difficult because the parenting itself creates self-doubt. Combine this with family members who tell you that your version of events is wrong, or that you're making a fuss, and then add society's general desire for you to respect your parents no matter what, and healing moves further and further out of reach. Recovering your ability to trust yourself is possible though. The more you let go of the need for other people to agree with your version of events, the more deeply you will start to trust yourself. The more you consider how you feel, the more you will trust your feelings and take them seriously.

## THE WAY IT WAS

This exercise is designed to help you get more clarity on how you experienced your parents when you were growing up. The questions are deliberately broad and designed to help you collect more internal data on your childhood experiences. As you work through them, try to trust your instincts without interrogating yourself or minimizing how you feel.

- What three words describe your mother as you experienced her when you were a child?
- What three words describe your father as you experienced him when you were a child?
- What did you need from your parent(s) that you didn't get when you were growing up?

## THEY JUST DON'T GET IT

The parts of your childhood that were difficult for you are not up for debate. Yet often there is still part of you that hopes that your parents might acknowledge their part in your suffering, or that wishes that they had done so if you are no longer in relationship with them. When it comes to the effects of childhood experiences, what objectively happened is not really relevant. What matters is how you perceived, understood, and experienced it at the time. If it *felt* overwhelming for you, then it was. If you didn't *feel* like your parents could be trusted not to hurt you, that's enough to make it so. If your family home *felt* hostile or chaotic, then that *is* how it was for you (because that's how your nervous system experienced it). Yet we can still get into debates with family members – and ourselves – about whether or not it was true.

Often when parents do or say something unkind or damaging to their children, it's because they are either acting unconsciously and repeating old interactions from their own past, or in a high state of stress and speaking from a state of fight-or-flight.

In both scenarios they are unlikely to be present, aware, or connected to themselves in these moments, and their memory certainly won't be at its best. Chances are that what you experienced as a child in a conversation with your parent, and what you recall of that now, is going to differ a lot from what your parent experienced at the time, and what they remember now.

Children experience their parents' words and actions in a unique way because they are experiencing the world in a different state to adults. All children, especially up until the age of seven, are operating in a theta brainwave state. This is like the mind's 'soaking sponge' mode, and it makes us deeply open and receptive to our experiences and environment. It's often compared to being in a hypnotic state because we're operating at a highly subconscious level. This is why those early years are such a time of incredible learning and growth. However, it also means that you would have been absorbing all of your interactions with your parents – their words, stress, reactions, and emotions – without any filter or buffer.

Children are also engaging with their parents from an inherently vulnerable position. Parents of young children and adolescents wield a disproportionate amount of power – not only because the child needs the adult to survive, but also because the adult is bigger and stronger. If an adult criticizes, mocks, or harshly disciplines their child, it will be a far more significant event for the child than it is for the adult.

What you felt during your childhood years, and the ways in which you experienced your parents, does not need be agreed upon or fact-checked by your parents to make it valid. Your parents are unlikely to remember things the way you do, because their actions would likely have occurred in an unconscious blur. They are also more likely to recall the positive or neutral moments between you, because this is less threatening to their sense of self. None of this is an excuse for that behavior, but it is an explanation for why your parents may interpret your childhood years very differently to how you do. Of course, it makes sense to want your parents to understand your point of view, and take some responsibility. However if, as for so many adult children of emotionally immature parents, this is not possible, you can still heal.

In the survey I ran with my online community that I mentioned above, I asked the participants: 'Have you discussed your feelings about your childhood with your parents? If so, what was the general outcome?'

Here are some of the responses:

- 'I sent my mother a letter about my feelings on my childhood and she just spoke of how it made her feel, which was case in point.'
- 'Only with my mum, once or twice verbally, once in writing. Each time I was met with, "Of course everything is my fault, I'm the worst mother," or the silent treatment... So I've stopped trying.'
- 'I have told my dad how much his behavior has affected me, but he didn't take it seriously or accept it and said I was making a monster out of him. I could never tell my mum how her parenting has affected me.'
- 'No outcome. They think they did their best.'

It's important that you use your energy wisely when trying to rebuild the parts of yourself that have been eroded by childhood. Now may be the time to release yourself from wanting your parents to acknowledge their actions and to validate your childhood experiences. Your energy is precious and better spent elsewhere.

## THE MYTH OF THE DIFFICULT CHILD

Emotionally immature parents often define one or all of their children as being difficult or hard work. What this really means is, 'My child was different to me and I didn't have the skills to understand them.' Parenting is by nature challenging. It's really the process of getting to know another human deeply, learning to accept what you find, and offering them love no matter what (plus providing countless meals and snacks, tidying, playing, making decisions for them, and so on). It is a difficult gig from day one. There's nothing wrong with finding it difficult to be a parent. There's also nothing wrong with a parent finding one of their children's temperaments more challenging than another's. However, there is something wrong with that parent not recognizing that the issue lies with them, and that *they* are the one who needs to adjust and adapt and reflect on themselves, rather than expecting their child to be the one to adapt to them; herein lies the emotional immaturity.

Parents are not owed children who neatly fit with their own traits and sensibilities. I say this as a parent of two children with very different temperaments. It is always the parent's job to figure out how to be the mother or father that that individual child needs. All babies, infants, and children differ and present their own unique challenges. It is the emotional immaturity of a parent that prevents them from responding to their child as they are, rather than as they want them to be. Invariably, when a parent significantly struggles with their child it's because that child is reflecting something in them that they haven't accepted or acknowledged. The child is triggering an unmet need or underlying belief that the parent has formed as a result of their own childhood.

If, for instance, a parent who hasn't been allowed to cry or feel sad as a child finds themselves with a very emotionally expressive or sensitive child, it's going to trigger them every time their child cries, or seems unhappy or dissatisfied. Because the parent wasn't allowed to express these emotions themselves as a child, they didn't get the chance to develop an understanding relationship with sadness, so parenting a sensitive child is going to be harder for them than it might be for someone else, and it will take work on their part to be able to meet that child's emotional needs. If they don't accept the challenge of self-work and self-reflection, there will likely be something missing in that parent-child relationship, causing distance, conflict, or repeated frustration on both sides. An emotionally mature parent responds to a challenging child and says, 'They are different from me and I need to figure out a way to understand them.'

■ ■ ■ ■

I'm so sorry if you spent your childhood triggering your parents. This makes for a difficult and damaging start in life. If there was something about your temperament that they found difficult, it was your parents' job to figure this out and to work on themselves enough to make sure that you didn't have to deal with their frustration, rejection, or disconnection. If they had done that work, they would not only have been able to parent you in the way that you deserved, but they would also have met a new and important part of themselves. Please know that it was your parents' lack of emotional insight and awareness that made parenting so difficult for them, and their inability to reflect on their own childhood is what led them to think you were the problem. But they were wrong, and it was *never* your fault. Now it's time to think about how your parents inadvertently created a whirlwind of inner turmoil for you (among other things) by understanding the types of wounds that emotionally immature parenting can create.

# CHAPTER 3
# UNDERSTANDING YOUR PARENT WOUND

Not long after I received my psychotherapy qualification, I began sessions with Chris, a 29-year-old man who was experiencing high anxiety, depression, and a crisis of life direction. His long-term relationship had recently ended, his career as a sports journalist was grinding to a halt, and he had had to leave his sociable life in London and move back home to live with his mother in the suburbs. He was terrified of the future and, it transpired, haunted by his past.

As we explored how his difficulties in childhood overlapped with his issues now, as an adult, I asked him something I ask many of my clients, which is to describe in three words how he experienced his parents when he was growing up (we looked at this in the exercise on page 33). The three words he used to describe his father when he was growing up were: angry, disinterested, disappointed. The relationship had left him feeling almost constantly not good enough. His mother had been an ineffective protector against his father's aggression and criticisms, and she fell into the 'everything's fine' parent category (*see pages 10–11*). The three words he used to describe his mother were: soft, weak, passive. He recalled her often telling him to 'stop winding Dad up' as she accommodated her husband's feelings while urging Chris to stay emotionally neutral. His parents split when he was 13, and seeing his father develop a close bond with his stepson when he remarried was confirmation (in Chris's eyes) that there was something fundamentally wrong with *him*.

Chris didn't get the safety and security he needed from his father, and he didn't get the support that he needed from his mother. These gaps left him feeling insecure and terrified of rejection as he started to craft his own life as an adult. His parent wound left him with the belief that he was not good enough. Not good enough to be respected or protected. Not good enough to be cared for or loved as he was. He therefore found himself in relationships with women who were emotionally unavailable and dismissive (a painful dynamic for someone who craved more reassurance than most). Chris's career, friendships, and life choices were all molded by his belief that he was defective, and his fear of being abandoned and rejected. His emotions ruled much of his life because he'd never been taught how to cope with them, so he used what he could (usually alcohol or food) to try to self-medicate, to pause his internal roller coaster and block out painful thoughts. The emotional wounds that were inflicted on him by his parents' lack of awareness, empathy, and conscious parenting affected almost every area of his life.

## YOUR PARENT WOUND

The parent wound is the gap between what you needed from your parents and what they were able to give you. This gap is where negative beliefs about yourself grow. It's where self-doubt and low self-esteem form. It's where emotions become a scary experience instead of a useful part of life. It's where relationships become painful and unhealthy. The gap is what makes the glass of life go from half-full to half-empty, because when your parents aren't able to meet your needs enough of the time, life becomes a struggle. The parent wound is ultimately recycled trauma; the unconscious passing down of fear, sadness, and regret, and the product of having parents who let their personal battles take center stage when you needed them to put you center stage for a while.

The mother and father types of parent wound are specific to your experience with each parent.

### Mother Wound

The mother wound often affects how you feel about yourself. Typically, mothers provide nurture, care, and acceptance, a place of emotional rest and sanctuary (ideally), and if this is not delivered well or consistently, it can make it difficult to care for or about yourself as an adult. Children with emotionally immature mothers often become adults with low self-worth. Your mother is your mirror, and the one you look to for confirmation that you are worthy of being fed, held, soothed, and loved, without condition. If instead, however, she pulled away, rejected you, or made her feelings seem more important than yours, or wanted you to become a mini version of her instead of your own person, it deeply affects how lovable and worthy you feel. Cue years of people-pleasing, low self-esteem, patchy self-care, and abandoning yourself.

## Father Wound

The father wound is considered to be slightly different in nature and impact. This is largely because children are, broadly speaking, likely to look to their fathers for qualities such as protection and guidance rather than nurture. When a father is absent (emotionally or physically) or overbearing, it leaves the child feeling unsafe, unprotected, unloved, and unworthy of male attention. This can lead to a desire as an adult to seek validation from other people or through external means (career, achievements, money, relationships), triggering an exhausting cycle of trying to prove yourself in lieu of a father who could see how much you are worth.

There are a further **five types of parent wound** that often develop more broadly from emotionally immature parenting. Learning about them will hopefully get you closer to understanding how your childhood is causing issues for you now, so that you can become less bogged down by your past. First, we'll talk about what forms these wounds take, then we'll try some exercises to heal and lighten their load.

## 1. Abandonment Wound

This wound is caused by feeling discarded, unwanted, or left, and by a childhood lacking in emotional warmth and nourishment. This might have been through literal abandonment (a parent leaving, being absent, or having minimal contact with you during your childhood), or through feeling brushed aside or ignored due to a parent's day-to-day actions or inactions. This tends to create anxiety as an adult, especially in relationships, which are often consumed with trust issues. It can also lead to chronic feelings of loneliness and a hypervigilance to signs of being abandoned by people. It affects your ability to form close, healthy relationships with people because of the fear of being abandoned, which makes intimacy and connection feel threatening.

If you have this wound, you might experience one of the following struggles as an adult:

- inexplicable sadness
- the need to be taken care of
- seeking reassurance and ongoing support and advice from people
- anxiety about being left out by friends or left by partners
- a tendency to merge with other people in relationships
- terror of being lonely/loneliness, even when you are with people

## 2. Humiliation Wound

This wound occurs when you feel ridiculed, embarrassed, or belittled as a child. It can be caused by a parent who mocked or shamed you, especially when you were enjoying yourself or trying to perform: 'You're being silly,' 'That's not right,' 'That's ridiculous.' When you experience this from your parents there is a significant impact on your self-worth, and it typically leads to low self-esteem, feelings of shame, and feeling that you are a bad person. You're also likely to feel embarrassed easily, and often feel judged by people.

If you have this wound, you might experience one of the following struggles as an adult:

- scared of being 'too' excited or having too much fun
- taking care of others to your own detriment, due to fear of being judged as selfish
- a tendency toward depression, due to a loss of trust in people and the world
- finding freedom and choice overwhelming
- feeling inadequate or not good enough
- keeping yourself busy to avoid the feeling of freedom (fear of a lack of boundaries)
- feeling (secretly) superior to others
- difficulty relaxing and enjoying life

## 3. Rejection Wound

The rejection wound occurs when you feel you are not accepted as you are as a child. Rejection wounds stem from experiences of being ostracized, criticized, left out, or invalidated. These leave the child feeling unloved or unwanted, which triggers a fear-based response. Being rejected by your parent, who you depend on, feels scary! The rejection wound leads to feelings of low self-esteem and a hypersensitivity to criticism. Other effects are a deep fear of rejection and feelings of unworthiness, making it difficult to establish healthy relationships.

If you have this wound, you might experience one of the following struggles as an adult:

- staying quiet or hidden
- people-pleasing
- a tendency to withdraw
- excluding yourself in social situations
- feeling different from others
- perfectionism and social anxiety
- feeling like you don't belong or fit in
- escapism (alcohol, drugs, food, video games, fantasies)

## 4. Betrayal Wound

This wound occurs when you experience a breach of trust as a child, such as the repeated breaking of small promises, a parent's infidelity, or a parent not protecting you. It is also caused by being frequently let down or manipulated, or consistently not having your expectations met by your parents. It can make it difficult to believe people, trust others, or form close connections with people due to an ongoing fear of being betrayed. It feels hard to be yourself around people because that leaves you feeling vulnerable, and small incidents of betrayal can take a long time to recover from.

If you have this wound, you might experience one of the following struggles as an adult:

- high expectations of others
- being on guard and defensive (including of your reputation/what others think of you)
- a desire to be important and useful
- suspicious of people/difficulty trusting people
- blaming other people easily
- seeking fame or wealth
- fear of being taken advantage of and difficulty being authentic or vulnerable with people as a result
- a desire to be right and for others to agree with you

## 5. Wound of Injustice

The wound of injustice is caused by feeling that you were being treated unfairly or that you were being denied what you considered fair as a child. It is also the result of experiencing cold or controlling parenting, in which you didn't feel free to do what you needed or wanted to do. The wound of injustice can occur if you felt unfairly treated in comparison to a sibling or if you weren't allowed to be yourself in your relationship with your parent. This wound often leads to anger and resentment, and can create a heightened sense of morality and fairness for yourself and others. It also means you create high standards, sometimes just for yourself but sometimes for others, too. The wound of rejection is always present behind the wound of injustice.

If you have this wound, you might experience one of the following struggles as an adult:

- perfectionism and a desire to conform to the ideals you've established in your mind
- rigidity about what is 'right' and 'wrong'
- a feeling that love and acceptance come when you do things well, meaning life is busy
- feeling lazy when you are relaxing
- finding it very hard when you make a mistake
- refusing help and being hyper-independent
- a focus on knowledge and logic over feelings
- sensitivity to perceived injustices and inequality in life, society, and relationships

## HEALING THE WOUNDS

Wounds are painful; they leave us vulnerable because they are still open and in need of care and attention. Untreated wounds affect us daily as we try to navigate life with this sore, unprotected part of us. When we do what's needed to heal the wound, it will start to close and will affect us less day to day. At this stage, nature helps us along and starts doing the natural work of healing, regenerating, and restoring. Eventually the wound closes and becomes a scar. Life can be lived well with scars. A scar is no longer a place of vulnerability in the same way as a wound is. We might remember what caused the original wound, but we're no longer in the trenches of the pain that it once caused. Scars can also fade over time and often become part of the texture of our skin, just as the experiences that caused the original wound become part of the texture of our life.

The following exercise is designed to help you increase your understanding and awareness of the nature of your parent wound, so that the healing process can begin.

## KNOWING YOUR PARENT WOUND

Which of the five wounds above (Abandonment, Humiliation, Rejection, Betrayal, Injustice) did you resonate with *most*? In this exercise, you can work through more than one, but start with the one that feels most like you. The questions invite you to think about your childhood, but if you've had a relationship with one or both of your parents as an adult, you can also pull on that for reference, especially if your memories of your childhood are unclear. Take your time doing this exercise. Your responses can be as detailed as you wish. Once you have fully explored the questions, preferably writing your answers down, you can start to think about which of the practices you can do, to start healing your wounds.

### 1. Abandonment Wound

– Brainstorm anything you recall about your relationship with your parents that led to you feeling left, overlooked, or unloved?

  For example: My dad was away working a lot and didn't seem that pleased to see me when he got home. My dad got angry with me and my sister a lot and my mum didn't do anything to help or defend us.

- How does this play out in your romantic relationships now?

  For example: I get really anxious when I start dating someone and find it hard to relax and enjoy the relationship. Or: I still worry a lot about my partner cheating or leaving, and feel so hurt after we argue that it takes me days to recover. I'm triggered and can't relax whenever he goes away with work, and I find myself imagining life as a single mum and feeling worried until he gets home.

### *Practices to Heal the Abandonment Wound*

- Resist filling your time and create intentional pockets of alone time.
- Aim to maintain your interests in spite of new romantic relationships or friendships.
- Develop a stronger sense of self by finding hobbies that bring you a sense of joy, peace, or well-being.
- The abandonment wound can be helped by healing your nervous system (*see Chapter 9*) and managing your anxiety. It's a fear-based wound that is both triggered by and perpetuated by high anxiety. Start to work practices into your life to help increase your resilience to stress and anxiety (breathwork, singing, yoga, meditation, time in nature).

### *Affirmations to Help Heal the Abandonment Wound*

- 'I am enough as I am.'
- 'Other people do not dictate if I am worthy or not.'
- 'I am safe in relationships and I am safe without romantic relationships.'

## 2. Humiliation Wound

- As far as you can remember, how did your mother or father react when you were excited, loud, playful, or boisterous as a child?
- Do you recall any times when you were ridiculed or belittled by a family member when you were growing up? If this came from a sibling, how did your parents respond?
- In what ways do you think your fear of being humiliated, embarrassed, or shamed has affected your life so far?

### *Practices to Heal the Humiliation Wound*

The humiliation wound is shame-based and one way you might unconsciously be trying to manage it is by staying productive and busy in order to feel of value. As part of healing, practice working small periods of unstructured time into your day to 'be' instead of 'do,' and to make space for relaxation.

Here are some examples:

| Being (the present; acceptance) | Doing (the future; productivity; action) |
|---|---|
| Focusing on where you are now and what you're doing | Making plans |
| Writing to be creative | Completing a writing project to be productive |
| Reading for pleasure | Reading to learn something |
| Checking in with your mind and body to see what activity or practice you need right now | Ticking things off your to-do list |

## 3. Rejection Wound

- When do you recall feeling in the way, overlooked, shamed, or pushed away by your parents growing up?

  For example: My parents were both very consumed with work (which I understand as an adult) and I remember feeling so empty coming home to our nanny, who wasn't interested in me or in how my day was. I remember trying to play with my parents when they were around, but they were always too busy or tired.

- What was your mother's general response when you felt sad or angry when you were a child?

  For example: She seemed irritated when I was sad, and embarrassed when I was angry if we were around other people. If we weren't, she just left the room.

- What was your father's general response when you felt sad or angry when you were a child?

  For example: He hated it when I cried, and he got angry when I got angry.

### *Practices to Heal the Rejection Wound*

The rejection wound can be helped by building your self-esteem. Here are some practices that can help with this:

- Write down three things every day that you like or love about yourself. (This will start to require your brain to think positively about yourself.)
- Reframe self-judgmental thoughts: 'My legs are so huge' becomes 'My legs are strong and help me live my life'; 'I'm

useless at new things' becomes 'I'm capable of growth and can be patient with myself.'

- Practice setting and holding boundaries; for example:
    - 'I'm not willing to talk about that.'
    - 'I won't be able to help you this time. I hope you find someone who can.'

## 4. Betrayal Wound

- Did one or both of your parents actively breach your trust or betray you or your family directly? For example, through infidelity, leaving the family, or breaking a big promise.

  For example: My parents would often have big arguments and my father would leave the family home for a week or two at a time. I never knew where he went or if he'd come back, and I remember having a sick feeling the whole time he was gone.

- In what ways do you think your betrayal wound plays out in your relationships now?

  For example: I'm often suspicious of my partner with other men/ women and find it hard to fully trust them even though we've been together for years. I often feel like the relationship is more hassle than it's worth because I constantly worry about what they're doing when I'm not with them, which is exhausting.

### *Practices to Heal the Betrayal Wound*

The betrayal wound often triggers a defensiveness and a need to be correct. Deliberately allowing people to misunderstand you will help to reduce this aspect of the betrayal wound. Practice noticing when people have misunderstood something about you, or something you're trying to do or say, and rather than trying to explain it further or convince them otherwise, let them be wrong, and stay grounded in what you know to be true about yourself.

## 5. Wound of Injustice

- If you have siblings, did you ever feel unfairly treated in comparison to them as a child (or as an adult, if you can't remember childhood clearly)?
- When you see someone else being treated unfairly or unjustly, how does it make you feel?
- What are the pros and cons of your difficulty with accepting unfairness or injustice?

  For example:

  **Pro:** I advocate naturally for people who need my help.

  **Con:** I find it really hard to get over how I feel when someone treats me or someone I know badly.

  **Pro:** I act morally and avoid causing other people harm.

  **Con:** I'm frequently burned-out and exhausted by the high standards I set for myself.

### *Practices to Heal the Wound of Injustice*

Start to notice when you are judging a person or situation based on what *you* think is right or wrong. Practice gently challenging your assumptions – not because your judgments are incorrect, but because you have the option not to break situations down into what is right and what is wrong. Remind yourself of the other aspects of the situation, such as what is beautiful about it, what is actually happening, whether it's something you need to give much thought to.

I hope this chapter has deepened your understanding of how the parenting you experienced has created patterns in your life now. As we continue connecting the dots between your childhood and your present life, we're going to move on to tackling the topic of trauma. It's a word that's used a lot, and a concept that's misinterpreted and misunderstood even more, so let's take a look at what trauma really means in the context of childhood and emotionally immature parents.

# CHAPTER 4
# HOW TRAUMA CHANGES US

Being raised by emotionally immature parents is a form of childhood trauma. However, 'trauma' is a word that feels heavy and serious, and for that reason it's a label that people are hesitant to connect to their own experience, especially when they've had an 'it looked good from the outside' kind of childhood. The word trauma conjures images of anything from severe car accidents to people trying to survive war. In comparison, Mum calling you fat and criticizing your outfit, or Dad coming home from work in a passive-aggressive mood most nights of the week, seems mild and unworthy of the trauma label. In trauma literature, there is constant reference to emotional trauma being defined as an event that felt overwhelming or out of your control. Trauma is a subjective, internal experience and so there is no checklist to verify what does and doesn't constitute trauma. Instead, as Gabor Maté says, 'Trauma is not what happens to you; it is what happens inside you as a result of what happens to you.'[1]

Maté writes that trauma is a spectrum and that distressing events can be separated into 'small t' trauma and 'big T' trauma. The effects of emotionally immature parenting typically fall into the category of 'small t' trauma. 'Small t' traumas are ongoing and cumulative, gradually eroding your sense of safety, self-worth, and security. They can be thought of as the impact of the needs we had that weren't met (with 'big T' trauma relating to the significant, harmful events that did happen). Needs like being accepted, being free to express your emotions, being seen, or being heard. If these needs aren't met in childhood, it results in trauma that goes on to affect your sense of who you are and how safe it is to be yourself. 'Small t' traumas can be harder to recognize and make sense of because they are not obvious and it takes some self-reflection to recognize them.

## HOW TRAUMA CHANGES THE BRAIN

Of course, painful experiences can happen at any age and stage of life, so why focus so much on the childhood ones? Why does childhood trauma get a category all to itself? Why are difficult childhood events considered different somehow to very painful life events that happen to us as adults? The reason is the long-term impact childhood trauma has on the brain, which makes the effects last years, decades, and sometimes a lifetime. The human brain is built during childhood: 'Overall growth of the brain is very rapid in the first years of life. Brain volume is about 35 percent of adult volume by 2–3 weeks after birth, doubles from term size in the first year of life and increases an additional 15 percent in the second year of life to about 80 percent of adult size.'[2] After the age of two, the brain continues to grow throughout childhood and adolescence and is thought to become more stable and set by the age of 26. (However, it is an organ and therefore the brain can still change throughout your life.)

Childhood experiences impact how your brain pathways are established, which affects the way you think, understand, connect with people, and process information and emotions when you are an adult. What happens to and around you as a child (and what doesn't happen that needed to happen) affects the rest of your life – until you heal.

It can, however, still be hard to reconcile your parents' arguments (which were so common you stopped consciously noticing them) – or the barbed comments your mother made, or your dad's moods that left you walking on eggshells whenever you were at home – with trauma. The research review 'Enduring Neurobiological Effects of Childhood Abuse and Neglect'[3] looked at the effect of difficult experiences in childhood on the brain. The categorization of childhood maltreatment in the review included the following:

> Verbal abuse, manipulation (e.g. placing the child in situations intended to elicit shame, guilt, or fear in order to serve the emotional needs of the perpetrator)… emotional neglect (failure to provide for the child's basic emotional needs). Emotionally neglectful parents may be emotionally unresponsive to a child's distress, fail to attend to the child's social needs, or expect the child to routinely manage situations that are beyond his/her maturity level.

There is a clear crossover between this definition of childhood maltreatment and emotionally immature parenting: namely, a parent-child relationship in which the needs of the parent are front and center, and the needs of the child are miscalculated or absent. The study found that the childhood experiences described have 'been repeatedly found to be associated with alterations in brain structure and function... Childhood maltreatment is associated with consistent alterations in corpus callosum, anterior cingulate cortex, dorsolateral prefrontal cortex, orbitofrontal cortex and adult hippocampus.'

The significance of these terms is that they refer to specific areas of the brain which play important roles in our brain function, as explained in this glossary.

## BRAIN GLOSSARY

Corpus callosum = processing information and brain health

Anterior cingulate cortex = problem-solving and decision-making

Dorsolateral prefrontal cortex = memory, planning, and organizing

Orbitofrontal cortex = decision-making

Adult hippocampus = memory, learning, emotions, and hormones

A 2021 review on depression and anxiety found that childhood trauma was associated with 'higher levels of neuroticism [anxiety] and negative self-associations, as well as lower levels of extraversion and optimism.' It was also associated with stress system dysregulations. From all childhood trauma types, emotional abuse and/or emotional neglect seemed to show the most profound effects.[4] A different study on the link between childhood trauma and depression states: 'Childhood trauma is a potent risk factor for developing depression in adulthood, particularly in response to additional stress.'[5]

These studies, and many others like them, prove that childhood trauma, and parenting that is emotionally neglectful or abusive, changes us. It changes the way our brains work. It changes the way we think and make decisions, and organize our time and lives. It alters how we show up in the world and how we connect, or don't connect, with other people. This is why it's important to take yourself and your experiences and your healing seriously; just because you had enough food, lived in a nice area, unaffected by war, famine, or natural disasters, and got a decent education, it doesn't mean you didn't have experiences that negatively affected how you and your brain developed.

## NATURE'S GIFT THAT WE DIDN'T ASK FOR

After the Twin Towers collapsed in 2001, a team of clinicians at Icahn School of Medicine at Mount Sinai, in Manhattan, assessed people who had been in the area, including 187 pregnant women. These women were tracked during pregnancy and beyond, with particular focus on symptoms of post-traumatic stress disorder (PTSD).[6]

Nine months later, they examined 38 of these women and their babies. Many of the mothers had developed PTSD and they also had unusually low levels of cortisol (something that researchers now associate with PTSD). Cortisol is a hormone that helps your body cope with stress, and too much or too little of it can have significant negative effects on the body.

The fact that some of the women who'd witnessed the traumatic collapse of the towers had developed PTSD is not surprising. However, the saliva of the babies of the women with PTSD also showed low levels of cortisol. It was concluded that their mothers' experience of trauma when they were *in utero* had changed the babies' stress-regulation systems. They were biologically changed because of their mothers' trauma.

We know that lesser traumas and stress in pregnancy leave their marks as well. A study published by the University of Colorado pulled together research on the effects of stress in pregnancy. This included moderate stress (such as life events and changes) and mild stress (such as small daily hassles). In the majority of cases, it was shown that mild, moderate, and severe stress can have negative influences on pregnancy outcome and the behavioral and physiological development of offspring.[7]

One way to understand how and why trauma gets passed down through the generations genetically is through epigenetics. Epigenetics is the study of how our genes are affected by our environment and explains how our experiences from conception and throughout childhood affect us long term. We are all born with genes inherited from our parents (informed by the generations before them) that guide our development, not only physically but also emotionally and in terms of our mental health. However, these genes can be activated, altered, or switched off by environmental factors, a process that happens more easily in childhood. How safe we feel in our early years, how attached we are to our parents, and how well our needs are responded to as infants all affect how our genetic makeup plays out.

For instance, you might be genetically predisposed to addiction; however, if you experience a generally emotionally safe environment as a child, with good attachments to your parents, and you receive parenting that helps you develop a high level of emotional awareness, intelligence, and stress tolerance, then you are less likely to experience addiction as an adult. Conversely, if you are genetically predisposed to addiction and you find yourself with parents who don't understand your emotional world and who can't offer emotional stability and guidance, then it's much more likely that that genetic predisposition will be activated.

However, the good news is that, in spite of our genes and early environment, we can always make changes and become more emotionally well adjusted by creating a different external and internal environment for ourselves. 'While some epigenetic marks are inherited or set during organismal development, many exhibit plasticity in response to the environment, allowing molecular adaptation throughout life… Large differences are observed in later life suggesting a substantial input from the environment during subsequent years.'[8]

In summary, epigenetics tells us that:

- Our ancestors' traumatic experiences can be passed down and imprinted in our DNA from birth.

- The parenting we receive and the environment we grow up in affects how our DNA behaves and how our genetic makeup plays out over the course of our lives.
- We *can* change how much of an effect our inherited traits have on our lives.

The fact that our genes can carry echoes of our ancestors' trauma is one of nature's gifts, albeit one that's somewhat of a mixed blessing. It can be seen as an attempt to prepare the next generation to cope better with their environment by tweaking its DNA. This would be useful if we were needing to survive the *same* environments, relationships, and challenges as our ancestors – but this is rarely the case.

In the modern world, we have an opportunity to live lives of good quality, in a way that many of our predecessors didn't. Their lives were often about survival (and the fact that they worked out how to survive is what allows us to be here in the first place) – and we rarely need the same level of fear as our ancestors had in order to survive. However, it gets passed down anyway.

Emotional vulnerability is generally going to be more useful for you in your relationships than emotional disconnection and mistrust. However, a predisposition to these latter traits may be in your DNA, having served your ancestors well as they focused on protection instead of connection. For example, feeling relaxed is more likely to set you up for success than being 'on edge,' but you may have been left with the echoes of your great-great-grandmother's nervousness (which ensured she lived a low-risk, safe life). Although much is passed on genetically, equally impactful is the way in which you were parented and what you learned directly and indirectly from your family. The parenting we receive creates its own imprint on our psyche – teaching us how best to relate to other people and how to function as an individual.

## RECOVERING

Evidence that change is possible, and that recovery from emotionally immature parenting is a reality, is offered by neuroplasticity. Neuroplasticity is the brain's ability to rewire and effectively reset itself in response to your experiences. This was previously assumed to be something that could only happen in childhood, but we now know that neuroplasticity is a lifelong process. The hippocampus is a part of the brain that affects emotions, hormones, memory, and learning. It's also the part of the brain most directly affected by stressful childhood experiences, including not feeling attached to or safe with your parents. Benedetta Leuner and Elizabeth Gould write in their paper 'Structural Plasticity and Hippocampal Function': 'It is now generally accepted that the hippocampus remains structurally plastic throughout life.'[9] This is amazing news and means that childhood doesn't have to affect us forever.

Neuroplasticity is both our explanation for why our childhood experiences affect us long term and our evidence that recovery is possible. The brain is always changing in response to your environment and the practices and information you expose yourself to. As a child, you have very little control over this, but as an adult, you can take actions that will change the structure of your brain and therefore alter how you feel, the nature of your thoughts, what you do, and how you come to view yourself and life in general. 'The same adaptability that allows the brain to change in response to trauma also facilitates healing. This lifelong ability means individuals can recover from childhood trauma by creating new, positive, supportive experiences. By consistently engaging in desired behaviors and avoiding negative ones.'[10]

In order to cope with emotionally immature parents, you have to adapt. This means that by the time you reach adulthood, it's likely that you've developed layers of alternative ways of coping with people, and new ways of thinking about yourself and understanding your place in the world. These adaptations are how we manage the trauma of not getting our needs met by the only people in the world who are meant to care enough to meet them. Altering your sense of self is a way of coping with the trauma of not feeling seen, loved, or understood by your parents. However, none of this is who you are. The parenting you receive can affect your beliefs, thoughts, behaviors, and decisions, *but* it doesn't alter your core being. The process of recovery from childhood trauma means recovering the parts of you that had to be squashed in order to get through your early years. As you start to feel safer, and able to connect with your truest self again, your beliefs, thoughts, and decisions will naturally change and become more aligned to the creation of a full and peaceful life.

## FEELING LIKE YOU'RE STARTING BEHIND

Childhood trauma leaves us feeling lost and adrift. While we are working out how to patch up our leaky boat, build a working oar, and figure out which direction to sail in, it seems that other people are floating along smoothly in the right direction, having been gently helped out to sea and waved off by their families. As you glance back at an empty shore, or see it filled with people who bring distress instead of comfort, everyone else seems to have reliable family stood on the shore, waiting for them to return for support should they need it. Even as you get your boat moving, each wave knocks you so much harder than it does other people.

The feeling that childhood trauma leaves us playing catch-up can be hard to shake. As we've explored in this chapter, not getting your needs met in childhood affects how your brain develops. This has a knock-on effect on how efficiently you find a life path that feels like yours, makes healthy relationships harder to create, and can set you back by making states of depression and anxiety easier to slip into and harder to get out of. There's something so fundamentally unfair about this – that your parents and your childhood can have such a profound negative impact on the rest of your life.

So, how do we use this information to propel us forward rather than keep us stuck? Firstly, let's get in touch with some anger about it all. Anger might not be a great emotional state to live in 24/7, but it's a vital and powerful part of the process of healing. Anger can motivate you to advocate for, and ultimately demand, a better quality of life for yourself. As a therapist, mother, and daughter of emotionally immature parents, I believe fully and deeply in the following statements:

- It was unfair that you didn't have parents who could set you up for a life of emotional health and good self-esteem.

- I'm sorry that you've had to spend time, money, and energy healing yourself.
- What happened to your parents isn't OK, but nor is what happened to you because of it.
- I wish it had been different for you.
- I'm sorry that you've had to teach yourself as an adult how to process your trauma, build confidence, have good relationships, and maintain stable mental health.

Once you let yourself feel angry about the parenting hand you were dealt, it can become a really useful part of the process of healing. Feeling anger about something that happened to you that hurt you is healthy. If you find yourself stuck there, however, then keep reading and we will move on to different stages of healing that should make anger less of a feature after a while.

It's impossible to know exactly how your childhood changed you. You will never quite know in which ways the parenting you experienced has altered you, and you can never be certain of how it might have been different. There is both frustration and peace to be found in this. Acknowledging the anger and sadness of it all is where healing begins, not where it ends. It shouldn't have been the way it was *and* there's a way to make life OK now. You deserved better *and* you can find better for yourself now. Life could have been so different *and* it still can be.

## YOU WERE BORN TO HEAL

Healing is a natural process. It is innate in our life force as living creatures to move toward repair; nature shows us time and again that living organisms are wired for healing. Animals have developed many ways to heal themselves. Wolves and big cats lick their wounds and their saliva contains antibacterial compounds and enzymes that promote healing, while starfish are renowned for being able to regrow lost limbs and, in some cases, an entire new body. Even plants have self-healing capabilities, such as sealing off wounds or producing secretions to enable healing.[11]

The term 'ecological succession' describes how ecosystems naturally repair and restore themselves after disturbances like fires, floods, or human activity. Nature has the ability to heal itself when given the right conditions:

- **Mount St. Helens, Washington State:** After a massive volcanic eruption wiped out the ecology of this mountain in 1980, plants like lupines began reclaiming the land within years.
- **Chernobyl Exclusion Zone, Ukraine:** Despite massive radiation following the world's worst nuclear disaster in 1986, nature has reclaimed the abandoned city, with forests, animals, and biodiversity.
- **Coral Reef Recovery:** After bleaching events, coral reefs can regenerate over decades if conditions improve.

However, often nature doesn't simply restore itself to its previous state after a disruption – it adapts and often improves, resulting in a transformed landscape. After wildfires, forests often regrow with a more open landscape and with fire-resistant tree species, meaning the forest regenerates with a new ecosystem. When wetlands restore after human disruption, they don't return to their exact original state but develop different plant species, new water channels, and altered biodiversity.

When we think of the ways our childhood might have changed us and set us back, healing can seem out of reach or futile; however, perhaps there is a way to heal while embracing the ways we've been changed by our experiences. Rather than trying to find the version of you that might have existed if your childhood had been different, maybe there's a way to increase your capacity to incorporate the changes, accept them as part of who you are, and continue toward healing anyway. Life wants you to heal. The natural course of life is to repair, regenerate, and recover, given the right conditions, support, and opportunity. While emotionally immature parenting creates wounds and changes us in ways we might never know, the place your mind and body naturally wants to move toward is a place of healing and recovery.

■ ■ ■ ■

So far, we've looked at what emotionally immature parenting is and my hope is that you've developed a deeper understanding of your dynamic with your parents and the ways in which it's affected you. Awareness and understanding are a foundational part of healing, but now we will move on to the next stage – acceptance and grief. This is an often messy, confronting, and challenging part of the healing journey, but one that offers so many benefits on the other side. Accepting and grieving are the cornerstones of any healing process, and allow us to transform our suffering into something new, better, and more worthwhile. After accepting and grieving will come self-parenting, and then, ultimately, a much fuller, richer, and more well-lived life. But accepting and grieving must come first if those latter parts of healing are going to last. So, let's get started with the transformational step of releasing your parents from their titles of Mum and Dad, and truly seeing them as the people they are, outside of the role of parent.

# PART II
# ACCEPTING AND GRIEVING

## CHAPTER 5

# THE HEALING POWER OF SEEING YOUR PARENTS AS PEOPLE

When I was about seven years old, I remember my parents talking about the night they met at a bar in London and their (slightly different) versions of events. They talked about the decade that followed, involving travel, friends, and living in a lovely flat in west London. They reminisced about their lives and jobs at the time, and what it was like living together for the first time. I remember listening to these stories and feeling profoundly struck by the realization that my parents had had a whole life before I existed (no, it hadn't occurred to me before!) and that, in fact, they had their own individual lives before they existed as a couple. It's hard for children to imagine their parents before they existed, in a similar way that they can't conceptualize their teacher existing beyond the school (cue strange feeling when seeing your teacher walking round the supermarket!). The adults in a child's life quickly take on set roles, and parents tend to exist in their children's minds purely as 'Mum and Dad.'

When we see our parents as just 'Mum' or 'Dad,' it means we largely view their behavior in the context of our needs and expectations, and how able (or not) they are to meet them. It means we are invested in our mother being a certain way, or our father doing certain things, in a way that we don't look for from other people. This is entirely appropriate for children, who should absolutely be looking to their parents to fulfill certain roles and functions in their life. As children, we see our parents as otherworldly and separate from other people, because we depend on them in such a unique way, and seek levels of acceptance, love, and validation from them that only they can provide. We are invested as children and adolescents in *not* seeing our parents' vulnerable, human side. We want to see them as capable parents, not as people with their own issues. It would be deeply unsettling as a dependent child to live with an active sense of your parents' trauma histories and difficulties with having relationships, for instance, and we work hard as children to see past their mistakes, issues, and weaknesses, so that we can continue to believe that they are capable of providing us good and stable care.

However, in adulthood, maintaining this view of our parents is counterproductive and ultimately stops you healing. When a parent-child relationship is relatively functional and healthy there comes a point – usually in adolescence – at which the child shifts from seeing their parents as 'Mum and Dad' and instead starts to see them as their own people, with separate and distinct life experiences, histories, values, and identities.

Seeing your parents as people means you start to see them as separate from you, and you as separate from them. This instantly makes the dynamic less intense and more manageable, and allows you some useful distance, meaning you can be in the relationships but not take what they say too seriously or be too bothered about what they think of you. When you make the shift to seeing your parents as people, you also shift them out of the role of being the primary source of love, acceptance, and validation in your life, and into more of a background role, and therefore you can experience the relationship without feeling threatened or defensive. This level of healthy detachment is achieved through a process called individuation.

Individuation typically happens first in adolescence, and it's the point at which we form a stable sense of self. As you individuate, you gain a clearer sense of yourself as separate from your parents, friends, siblings, and others around you. Swiss psychologist and psychiatrist Carl Jung talked about the importance of individuation, and discussed it as a process of self-realization.[1] Individuation is essential if you are to live an emotionally healthy, stable adult life; however, when you've grown up with emotionally immature parents, it can complicate or stop the process of individuation happening.

When the relationship with your parents has been dysfunctional, codependent, or lacking in something significant, it makes it much harder to let go of them as parents psychologically, and to see them instead as people. Jung proposed that in order for individuation to occur in adolescence, it is necessary that there is belonging, a connection with the family that allows for a starting point, and an environment that facilitates the process.

If you didn't have a healthy connection to your parents, it makes the process challenging, or sometimes impossible.

## WHAT STOPS US SEEING THEM AS PEOPLE?

Seeing your parents as people involves loss. This is the case even when the relationship has been difficult or damaging. Harmful or not, your dynamic with your parents is still yours, and is familiar and embedded into you as part of your life story. Therefore, altering your concept of who your parents are means triggering the loss of who they have been to you. It also involves the loss of who they might have been as parents, requiring you to accept that you will never get to experience them as the parent that you needed. This can feel like a psychological waving of the white flag and giving up on what you've unconsciously been waiting for from them for all these years. This is painful for that part of you that can't quite accept that your parents were never able to be who you needed them to be.

It's also really difficult for your inner child, who is perhaps still waiting for them to change. There's a lot of waiting involved with having emotionally immature parents: waiting for them to become who you need; waiting for them to understand; waiting for them to grow and be different. Seeing your parents as people instead of your parents in many ways signals the end of waiting. It means you are no longer as invested in them being the parents you needed, and are more invested in becoming an emotionally healthy, separate self. This is liberating, but painful.

Emotionally immature parents and dysfunctional family systems tend to fear change, and there is no more fundamental change than changing the concept you have mentally held of your parents for decades. In enmeshed and codependent families, changing, growing, or choosing new over old is seen as a betrayal. The very process of letting go of the idea of who your parents are, and of who you are in relation to them, can feel disloyal. However, it's not disloyal to choose emotional health, mental well-being, and a better future for yourself. Seeing your parents as individuals is part of that process, and accepting their human frailties and flaws is a step toward emotional health for you.

## THEY DIDN'T DESERVE WHAT HAPPENED TO THEM, BUT NEITHER DID YOU

When you no longer see your parents as having let you down, damaged you with their comments, and failed to meet your needs, you are left with seeing their sadness instead. You're faced with understanding that your parents were traumatized too, and in this moment you're confronted with your family's generational trauma. The realization that your experience of your parents when you were a child didn't come from nowhere, and that, in fact, it sits in the context of your parents' childhood circumstances and the society they were raised in, and your grandparents' childhood circumstances and the society they were raised in, and so on, is a painful thing to confront.

It means accepting something that most children work extremely hard to deny or try to change: the reality that your parents were not always (or were perhaps very rarely) happy. The reality that your parents were not OK, and perhaps are still not OK. Part of healing from the trauma caused by your emotionally immature parents means accepting that they were traumatized too, and just as you developed ways to cope with your childhood, so too did they. This isn't an excuse for the pain they caused, but it is an important part of your healing – to understand and accept that your parents passed down to you what was passed down to them. Maybe not directly, but in some form. I have a very difficult relationship with my mother, and my relationship with my grandmother (my mother's mother) has always been a source of security and comfort to me.

To me my grandmother was kind, patient, and full of unconditional love. One of the hardest parts of my healing process has been acknowledging that my grandmother is very unlikely to have been able to give my mother what she needed as a child; to accept that my grandmother was likely emotionally immature when raising my mother. It's been hard to reconcile with *my* experience of my grandmother, but it wouldn't serve me to pretend that my mother's issues came from nowhere. As you develop more of an understanding of the intergenerational patterns of shame, suffering, suppression, and emotional deprivation that you may have been born into, you'll be able to step out of the pattern, so that you can create something new for yourself.

Facing the sad and unfair parts of your parents' lives also means that you're called to feel compassion, sympathy, or understanding for them and the difficult parts of their human experience. This is a big ask when they have contributed so greatly to the difficult parts of your human experience. However, healing is rarely smooth or easy, and so we must learn to find a way to acknowledge the painful, sad, or disappointing parts of our parents' lives, while still honoring and healing our own experiences. Being able to let the difficult parts of their story exist alongside the difficult parts of your story is powerful but challenging. It might involve seeing your dominant mother as a woman who became angry to cope with the injustice she experienced, rather than just a mother who shouted at you a lot. It might mean seeing your abusive father as a scared six-year-old boy, because chances are that's what he was (and perhaps that's how he felt when he was trying to parent you). None of this changes or lessens the impact of their actions on you, though, so how can you acknowledge your parents' trauma while still holding space and compassion for the trauma you faced because of them?

## THIS IS WHERE WE USE 'AND' INSTEAD OF 'BUT'

Instead of:

My mother was so hard on me, which has affected my life so much, but I know she had a hard time growing up so I should cut her some slack.

Reframe:

My mother was so hard on me, which has affected my life so much, and I know she had a hard time growing up, too.

Instead of:

Dad was always so defensive, but I know his dad had anger issues as well, so it must have been hard for him to stay calm.

Reframe:

Dad was always so defensive, which made it really hard for me to express myself, and I know his dad also had anger issues.

There's a level of acceptance that these kinds of reframes can help us reach. An acceptance of how your parents are, or were. It's important to note that accepting the way your parents are is not the same as accepting the way they treated you. Some behavior is unacceptable and nothing will change that; accepting the way your parents have been is simply a deep and conscious acknowledgment. An acknowledgment that your mum is critical or emotionally cold, and that there's nothing you could have done to change that. An acknowledgment that your dad struggles with emotions or can be controlling, and that this would have been the case no matter who his child was.

## MAKING THE SHIFT

Learning to see your parents as people, rather than as your mum and dad, is a healing catalyst. It's what takes you from being the one who experienced it, to being the one who worked hard to understand it and heal it. Developing an idea of what your parents' childhoods might have been like can help you develop more context and understanding of their life stories. Below are some questions to reflect on. This isn't an exercise of accuracy, but rather a way to deepen your general sense of your parents' psychological states and emotional lives. You may have no information at all to go on, in which case just sit with the questions and see what, if anything, comes up for you. You may, on the other hand, have a lot of information about what your parents' childhoods were like, in which case write down what feels most true and important for you.

– What was the emotional climate of your parents' childhood homes?

- How did your parents interact with their parents (if you ever witnessed this)?
- What effect might your parents' sibling relationships have had on them as they were growing up (if they had siblings)?
- How did your grandparents seem to deal with the core emotions of sadness, anger, and anxiety?

## YOU ARE NOT YOUR PARENTS

Part of being able to see your parents as individuals involves seeing yourself as an individual. This is particularly difficult if you grew up with codependent or enmeshed parents who required you to prioritize being a good daughter or son over being your own person (*see page 166–168*). Seeing your parents as people can't happen unless you also see yourself as someone who exists beyond the remit of your relationship with your parents or family, and yet our inextricable connection to our family is drummed into us from a young age:

- 'The apple doesn't fall far from the tree.'
- 'Like father, like son.'
- 'Like mother, like daughter.'
- 'She's my mini me.'
- 'He's a chip off the old block.'
- 'They're cut from the same cloth.'

When your relationship with your parents is generally good, the concept that you are like them, or destined to become like them, may be welcome (although it's also deeply codependent). However, when the relationship with one or both of your parents comes with pain, conflict, or confusion, the idea that you are the same as or similar to them can be harmful and make healing seem futile. There are many animal species who quickly separate from their parents soon after birth, forever or for long stretches as a baby, including turtles, sharks, lizards, and birds. They are born as sentient individuals, just as we are, but the difference is that those animals are born with everything needed to survive independently. As mammals, however, we are born dependent on other people, and in particular our mothers, for survival, meaning we have no choice but to assimilate with her and the rest of our family to grow and survive. Therefore, there will likely be similarities, learned and genetic, between you and your parents. You share DNA with your biological parents, which carries with it a predisposition to certain traits. You will also have learned ways of being – some subtle and some more significant – from seeing how your parents lived, and are likely to have developed some unconscious rules for living based on this.

However, it's also the case that you are an individual, with your own unique way of operating in the world and your own specific set of values: with your own soul, essence, and spirit. You were born dependent on other humans as we all are, but you were also born complete and whole, with your own beating heart, breathing lungs, and curious brain. The truth is that you *are not* your parents. You come from them, but you are not them. Healing asks that we hold two truths simultaneously:

- 'I share genes with my parents AND I have my own unique genetic makeup.'

- 'I have been affected by my parents AND I have always existed beyond my parents.'
- 'I developed in the context of my family system AND I am an individual.'
- 'I am connected to my parents in some ways AND completely unconnected in others.'

Individuation can happen at any age and although it ideally begins in adolescence, it is thought to deepen in mid-life. It's never too late to begin or deepen the process of seeing your parent as a person instead of as a mother or father. A person who had to learn how to cope with their childhood. A person who had big disappointments as a teenager, and traumas as a young adult. A person who has dealt with health issues, redundancies, heartbreak, depression, uncertainty. Seeing your parents as people is healing because, in the same way as they are no longer only a mother or father, you are no longer only a daughter or son.

■ ■ ■ ■

As you deepen your acceptance of who your parents are as people, we now move into accepting your childhood as a whole. This is a process of grieving what was lost, mourning what could have been, and working toward it becoming a small part of your story, rather than the main storyline. We'll look at acceptance and grieving in more detail – a powerful and vital part of any healing process.

# CHAPTER 6

# ACCEPTING AND GRIEVING THE HAND YOU WERE DEALT

A childhood without a deep connection to your parents is a childhood lived with a broken heart. Our parents are our first loves. We recognize our mother's voice before we even leave her womb.[1] We spend our first months on Earth studying our parents' faces. They are our entire world in those early years. We search for their gaze and reaction, a way to confirm that we exist, that we matter, and are worthy of connection and love. Being raised by a parent who couldn't see you, accept you, or love you fully is heartbreaking. Knowing that we don't get the chance to have a different childhood, with different parents, can be so painful to accept that it keeps us stuck in a limbo. A limbo of not quite wanting to accept the way it was. A limbo of hoping that it might change or wishing it could have been different. Accepting that you didn't have the parents that you needed is a painful part of healing; however, it's a necessary part. Acceptance allows you to live fully in reality rather than in an in-between space, wishing things were different, or pretending it was fine, or hoping your parents might change (if you currently have a relationship with them).

## WHY ACCEPTANCE MATTERS

Acceptance can be something we unconsciously block or avoid, because accepting the difficult parts can feel like losing hope. Hope is an important part of coping with emotionally immature parents. Whether it's hope that they will change, or hope that they will understand, or become different, or heal. Or hope that the relationship will get better, or that there will, in some way, be a happy ending after all. Hoping that your situation might improve as a child is a vital part of coping with emotionally immature parents; however, as an adult it can become part of what keeps you stuck. Accepting that your parents were not who you needed them to be involves letting go of the hope that things might improve (if you currently have a relationship with your parents). It also means letting go of the part of you that still fantasizes about a better childhood. There can, however, be a *transfer* of hope, rather than just a loss of it. Hope for a better future for yourself instead of hoping for resolution with your parents; hope for your future self, instead of wishes for your past self. Acceptance turns the impact of your parents' emotional immaturity from something that dominates how you feel about yourself into a relatively small part of your life. It moves it to the background. Acceptance moves you from despair to growth and a shift from feeling helpless to feeling empowered. Trying to heal without accepting the realities of what you are healing from is like building a house without solid foundations – acceptance is the part of healing that creates space for all the rest.

## WHY FORGIVENESS DOESN'T MATTER

Forgiveness is often heralded as the final destination for healing. The ultimate sign of having moved on. As a therapist, I've seen people try to force themselves to forgive someone who has caused them harm, striving to reach a point of neutral nirvana in relation to people and events that have significantly altered their world and sense of self, and that continue to cause them pain. Personally, I don't think forgiveness is an essential part of healing. It is my belief that some things are unforgivable. I'm also, however, not against the concept of forgiveness if it feels like a natural step, and in my experience the more you heal, the more you naturally transcend past experiences to such an extent that forgiveness will be an organic, almost unconscious process, as these painful experiences fall away from your day-to-day life and thoughts.

The main argument for forgiveness is that *not* forgiving someone means you are retaining a level of anger toward them which is harmful to *you*. I have found, however, that acceptance can have sufficient power to enable you to disentangle yourself from the experience, enough for it not to actively stay with you each day. It's also useful to note that in some circumstances and relationships, anger is entirely appropriate (and useful). If, for instance, you are still in a relationship with an emotionally immature parent who continues to act without awareness or emotional regard, it can be unwise to drop your defenses when you are with them. Anger, as with all feelings, is a signal. It's one of the ways your body tries to let you know that you may not be safe or that you need to protect yourself. This can be necessary when it comes to dealing with emotionally immature people, and anger is a core part of your gut instinct and intuition system. Anger can lead to vital boundaries being set, and trying to prematurely repress anger with forgiveness can be emotionally unsafe.

There are some times in life when you are called to forgive one isolated event – for example, if someone mistreats you on one occasion – which can feel manageable. However, when it comes to emotionally immature parenting, there are often so many moments, events, memories, and layers of hurt that have compounded over time, that forgiveness becomes unrealistic. Forgiveness can feel like a betrayal of self. If this is the case for you, and if it's blocking you from moving forward in your healing, it's OK to focus on acceptance instead.

Acceptance is simply a deep and conscious acknowledgment of your reality and experiences. It is necessary in order to clear enough psychological space to heal. Acceptance of how your childhood was, and how your parents were and have been, means a letting go of what never was, what couldn't be, and what will never be. It's a commitment to aligning with reality, no matter how painful or unfair that might feel. Acceptance doesn't mean it was OK – it is simply an adjustment to reality. Forgiveness doesn't have to be part of your healing process.

## THE LOST YEARS

I have dedicated most of my adult life to healing childhood trauma (whether doing so myself or helping others to) and yet I still remember how frustrating and unfair it felt, especially in the early phases of healing, that I needed to heal because of someone else's actions. It felt like someone dumping a giant bin full of rubbish onto your lawn, and you having to spend your whole weekend clearing it all up. This is how emotional healing can feel – only instead of a weekend, it's years and years.

There's also a painful phenomenon that sometimes occurs when you are relatively early on in the process of personal growth/awakening/transformation/healing (or whatever other description you might use), when the progress that you've made inadvertently highlights what you've missed out on in the years that have come before. The years before you became more conscious and aware. I think of these as the lost years, because often we are so deep in survival mode that we can't enjoy life, or take care of ourselves, or appreciate other people, or remember much of what happened before we started healing, and sometimes we do things in order to survive the lost years that we hate the thought of now (more on these coping strategies in the next chapter).

Grieving the lost years is a painful part of the journey, but being aware of them is a really positive sign. It means you are moving from one state to another. From unconscious to conscious. From survival mode to more present living. Let yourself be sad for those times in the past when all you could do was get through each day. The sadness will pass eventually and when it does, you'll be able to sink even more deeply into a life of presence and awareness.

Grieving the lost years can feel worse due to the fact that many people had parents who were generally able to meet their needs, or childhoods that felt safe and nurturing, and therefore don't have to spend years working on themselves. The way I have managed this reality is firstly by feeling rightfully angry about it, because it isn't fair and it does set you back in many ways. Secondly, I remind myself of what I call the 'Pilates rule.' In my late 20s, I had bad back and neck pain and was advised to try various things, including osteopathy and Pilates. I learned a lot about human anatomy and my body in particular, and discovered a body-management system that has meant that I very rarely get neck pain and haven't had any back pain at all for years. My body awareness is also much better as a result, which I'm sure has benefited me in various other ways, too. Conversely, I know people who were pain-free in their 20s, who didn't learn about how to care for their body, who didn't take up Pilates, and who now, years later, have pretty significant recurring neck pain and back issues. Having a problem that I needed to address meant that I became more aware of my body and learned how to take care of myself properly, which I wouldn't have done if I hadn't needed to heal my neck and back issues. The same can be said for those of us who have had to do the work of processing childhood trauma. It's an opportunity for you to dig way deeper than those who had a reasonably good childhood might need to, and in digging deeper you might learn how to take care of yourself really well, deal with your emotions in a healthy way, cope better with stress, and be grateful for life in a fuller and more complete way than those who have never had to heal. On the other side of healing is often a richer experience of life. Other people may have a smoother ride, but you will gain a bigger life.

## CLAIMING YOUR GRIEF

Accepting and grieving go hand in hand. A parent-child bond is built on the belief that your parent will always be available to you. This is what allows you to attach to them. However, if you lose your parent, be it through death, loss of contact, or through their lack of availability to you, it triggers grief. Grieving can occur for loss of any type, not just death. It also often happens in layers and on a different timescale than you might expect; for instance, you can experience delayed grief following an increased awareness of the different levels of loss involved in your childhood. You may have had no contact with a parent for years, but still not have grieved them fully. You might know that your parent has let you down repeatedly, but not have found a way to acknowledge the loss you feel. Although grieving your childhood feels like a daunting task, life tends to get much easier on the other side of grief.

Grieving serves as a release and provides relief. Grief is a concept usually reserved for the bereaved, which can make grieving your childhood difficult because other people don't acknowledge it as grief. This is grief that isn't triggered by the death of someone, but rather by a retrospective loss of the safety that you needed as a child, which makes it abstract and easy to ignore or delay. Other people won't get it, and you therefore won't get some of the empathy, patience, or space that those who are bereaved often get. It can feel particularly lonely to grieve your childhood. To accept your childhood as it was means to grieve the loss of what you *didn't* get. To accept your parents as they were (or are) means to grieve that they were not what you needed them to be. It means grieving the losses you experienced as a child and mourning the times when you needed emotional support, safety, or connection that wasn't available. It means grieving for what could have been, and saying goodbye to what you longed for that never materialized.

## GRIEVING THE LIVING

While mourning your experience of emotionally immature parenting, you will likely have the challenging task of grieving someone who is still alive. When I was 25, my father left the family home in the middle of the day, taking all his belongings, and never came back. I didn't hear from him at all after that day. It transpired he had been having a decade-long affair and had gone to live with this other woman and her child. I spent the next five years grieving my father, even though he was still alive. I decided to treat it as a death, because that is exactly what it felt like. So, I let the grieving happen. I let myself be depressed, I allowed the waves of sadness to wash in and wash back out again. I cried. I talked about it sometimes. I refrained from talking about it other times. I remember thinking how hard it was to grieve someone who was alive, because although people around me were aware of his sudden departure, I don't think many people realized that I had effectively experienced the death of a parent without the opportunity for a funeral. It was a death without the support or understanding that the bereaved are usually offered.

For the most part I would say I have moved through the grief, and I hear he has now passed away, which makes it more final. However, occasionally the sadness returns. Grief isn't necessarily a finite process. If you allow yourself to grieve your childhood, then there will be a period of intensity in which you feel it *acutely*. This stage won't last forever, but some feelings of sadness or anger might remain, cropping up from time to time. This is part of the human experience: to process pain and therefore no longer be affected by it day to day – but to occasionally have moments when it visits you again.

I have also grieved my mother, with whom I still have a relationship. I worked intensively on my mother wound (*see pages 43–44*) in my early 30s, when I was pregnant and in the early stages of motherhood. I mourned what I needed from her that wasn't available. I grieved the (temporary) loss of my authentic self that I felt as a daughter who was controlled, squashed, and worn down in the relationship. This type of grieving is a form of silent grief. There are few places it can be discussed. Few people (if any) will acknowledge it. There's no official death to reference, but it's a process of mourning to navigate nonetheless. One of the hardest parts of grieving someone who is still alive is that there is no space given for you to grieve – no bereavement leave, no relatives helping out with the children, no allowances made. When you are grieving the loss involved in having emotionally immature parents you must *claim space for yourself*. You must take it seriously and allow yourself time to process it. Give yourself space, give yourself time, give yourself grace, and give yourself the chance to grieve.

## HOW TO GRIEVE

If you haven't yet faced much of your grief about your childhood, the thought of opening the emotional floodgates might feel overwhelming. Know that you are built to grieve; loss is part of life and it features, in some small or large way, in every transition (life essentially being a series of transitions). You have an incredible inbuilt infrastructure to allow you to grieve and it really is a case of just letting it happen rather than actively doing something. Grieving happens alongside real life. It isn't something you can pause everything else to do, and you don't need to. In terms of the mechanics of emotional processing, we are designed to feel our emotions quite intensely, and then let them pass through us and leave (*see pages 114–119*). However, if you spent much of your childhood confronted with emotions you couldn't process, you probably developed lots of ways to avoid feeling or processing emotions at all. Grieving involves reclaiming your natural skill of emotional processing and allowing yourself to get in touch with some of the feelings that you couldn't face as a child – and feeling them now.

In order to allow ourselves to grieve, especially for something that happened years ago, we need to create a life that has room for grief. Life and all its tasks and demands can easily get in the way. So, what does a life that has space for grief look like? It's a life that isn't completely filled with tasks. That isn't exclusively about doing. A life with moments of stillness.

That's when the grief can enter. Of course, we need to get things done as well, but you may also need to give yourself that 15 minutes here and there to reflect and cry. I once had a client who had a busy corporate job and three children, who was also in the midst of healing her childhood trauma. She allocated herself grieving time in which, twice a week, she would bring to mind her inner child by looking at old photos, and cry for everything she didn't get and had to endure. During this time, she would find a place to be alone, and she would write to her inner child and deliberately bring painful memories to mind. This is how she managed to mourn while living her life. Other people process their childhood grief in one chunk each week in therapy, and some do so with damp, teary eyes stood in a post office queue after seeing a child laughing with their father in a café. I have always preferred 4 a.m. grieving sessions: this is the time at which my subconscious wakes me up when we have work to do. The work of crying, reflecting, wondering, thinking. Whatever works for you, do that. There is no right or wrong way to grieve; it's a natural process when we give ourselves permission.

Crying can provide enormous relief and is an important part of grieving. Dr. William H. Frey, a neuroscientist and biochemist, conducted research showing that emotional tears contain stress-related hormones like cortisol and ACTH. His studies suggest that crying helps the body eliminate these substances, reducing emotional stress.[2] Emotional tears contain higher concentrations of stress hormones and other proteins compared to reflex tears (tears from chopping an onion or getting dust in your eyes).[3] Crying, therefore, is a release. But it may be that crying doesn't come easy for you. You may have disconnected from your emotions to the point that you can't access them, or crying may be something that has unconsciously been off limits to you for some time. It can feel really frightening to let yourself cry if you're not used to it. It's likely to be deeply uncomfortable and there can be an underlying fear that you'll be taken over by your emotions. Usually, however, once you get through the initial waves that can indeed be big and forceful, the tide dies down. You'll be surprised how quickly you can move through the stage of grieving your childhood once you allow it to happen. Be patient with yourself. If you know that crying for your childhood needs to be part of how you heal, try exploring some of the questions to trigger grieving in the exercise below. Therapy can also be a great place to remember how to cry again, if you are able to access it.

What if, on the other hand, you've been crying for years and feel like you're getting nowhere? Grieving is a combination of feeling and thinking, emotionally releasing and cognitively sorting. It's entirely possible to cry a lot and also to be avoidant of emotion, and crying can become a behavior rather than a process of connecting with how you feel.

If you've been crying about your childhood for a long time and don't feel any further along in your healing process, it might be useful to consider whether you are crying without actually connecting to your emotions or processing your memories. When we process something, it means we are making sense of it little by little. It means that each time we cry or wonder or reflect, we are moving gently away from one state and toward another, no matter how small that shift may be. Each time you cry about your parents or your childhood, try to imagine releasing old feelings to make way for something new. Rumination is 'a thinking style characterized by a repetitive inward focus on negative cognitions.'[4] It's like being stuck on a hamster wheel with the same thoughts whirring around continuously. Processing, on the other hand, is a more active process, geared toward working through and making sense of something.

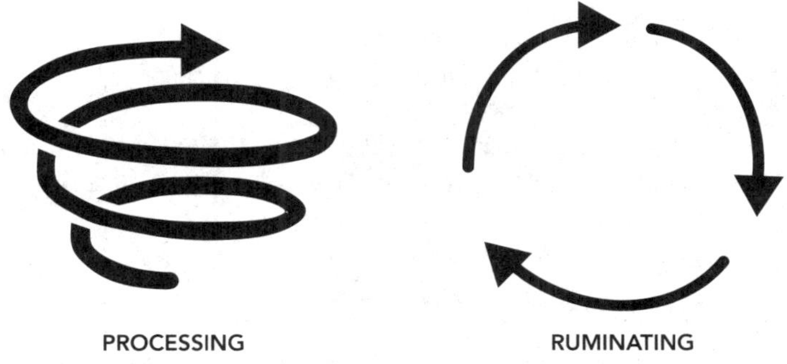


*Processing vs ruminating*

Combine crying with asking yourself questions and thinking about what happened, why, and what it means. You can feel your feelings fully *and* bring useful thoughts on board that will help you process your emotions, rather than recycle them.

## STARTING TO GRIEVE

These questions are designed to gently guide you toward deeper self-awareness and healing. I invite you to answer just two or three at a time, in some detail and at a time and place that allow you to connect emotionally with your answers. If you become overwhelmed by your feelings, remind yourself that healing happens in layers – it's okay to take breaks, seek support, or revisit these reflections over time. Take care of yourself as you grieve and be kind to yourself as you process.

- What memories do I have of feeling alone, scared, or unheard as a child?
- Were there times I felt like I had to grow up too fast? What did that look like?
- If I could rewrite my childhood, what would I change?
- When did I first realize my childhood was different from that of others? How did that feel?
- What did I have to suppress (playfulness, curiosity, trust) to survive my childhood?
- What did I need from my parents that they were unable to give me?
- Have I ever downplayed my childhood trauma? What would happen if I allowed myself to fully acknowledge it?
- If my childhood experiences had happened to someone else, how would I feel about them?
- When I see children who are loved, protected, and cared for, how do I feel? What does that tell me?

Take a moment to sit with these answers. Give yourself permission to feel whatever comes up – whether it's sadness, anger, or even relief. Your emotions are valid, and grieving is a necessary step toward healing.

## Putting Sadness in the Passenger Seat

After a childhood of being let down and emotionally abandoned by your parents, sometimes sadness will remain one of your companions in life – even when you've grieved. However, the more you accept and grieve your childhood, the less potent and present your sadness will be. It might still be there, but it will fade more easily and crop up less often. As you move through your grief, it's useful to start to move emotions like sadness, guilt, or fear into the passenger seat. All emotions are welcome and useful, but not all emotions deserve to be the driving force in your life. You are the driving force in your life, and your difficult childhood, and the emotions that go with it, are just one of the many passengers coming along for the ride.

■ ■ ■ ■

Over the last couple of chapters, we've talked about the acceptance of your childhood and of your parents, and now it only seems fair to extend the same grace and generosity to you. So, let's talk about acceptance of all the ways you've coped over the years in response to having parents who didn't give you what you needed emotionally. Everything you've done and not done, been and not been, said and not said. Let's look at it, understand it, embrace it, love it – and then release it.

# CHAPTER 7
# YOU MAKE SENSE

We must all find ways to cope with the environment we find ourselves in as a child. The way our parents speak to us, feel about us, respond to us, react to us, and treat us is one of the most significant parts of our environment as a child. We look to our parents to keep us safe, emotionally and physically, but when our parents' emotional immaturity means they can't keep us emotionally safe in the way that we need, we have to find ways to cope. So we test different ways as children to get our needs met: our need for love, guidance, connection, acceptance, nurture, and validation. The methods that work stick with us, and become coping strategies that follow us into adulthood. Coping strategies allow us to manage the anxieties that come with life: uncertainty, risk, judgment, criticism, love, loneliness, and rejection.

The ways people cope with life always makes sense in the context of their upbringing, and all coping strategies work to some extent. However, some people can be quick to judge others' coping strategies, not recognizing what radically different emotional environments we can be raised in. For instance, someone who pushes themselves at work and achieves success in their career by overworking is admired, whereas someone who isn't able to maintain a job and doesn't have financial or professional success can be dismissed as lazy. However, at the core of both may well be a critical parent whose words continue to occupy their thoughts. One tries to cope with the critical narrative in their head by overworking and overcompensating, while the other gives up before they've started, as a way to ward off the shame of trying and failing. Both are coping strategies. One is praised in society while the other is criticized.

We all develop coping strategies in response to how we are parented, but while some coping strategies are healthy and help us to grow, others ultimately keep us stuck. When you've developed your coping strategies in response to emotionally immature parents, the type of coping strategies may be on the unhealthy side, mainly because they are a reaction to unhealthy behaviors and are usually based on trying to get your needs met, needs that should be met by your parents. One of the markers of an unhealthy coping mechanism is something that helps in the short term but becomes a problem long term (and often becomes more and more of a problem as time goes on). For example, coping strategies like using alcohol, food, or drugs to help you numb your emotions. Or avoiding places, people, or situations that bring you anxiety. As you heal from emotionally immature parenting you may start to notice how you have coped over the years.

In the context of your childhood and the specific ways you responded to your environment as a child, all your past choices, behaviors, and ways of coping make sense. The ways you've been in relationships make sense. The things you've prioritized in your life make sense. The parts of your life that you've struggled with make sense. The decisions you've made make sense. They might not all seem good or correct, and you may have some regrets, but I promise you they all make sense based on your childhood, and the ways you had to adapt to your parents. You make sense. This doesn't mean that you are required to continue coping in the same ways. You are absolutely allowed to change. But after a lifetime of avoiding emotional intimacy, or tying your identity to your career, or hiding in motherhood, or drinking heavily, or eating to the point that you feel numb, or whatever else you might have done to cope so far, it can be difficult to imagine what life might be like if you stopped these things. What would be left?

## AUTHENTIC SELF

Emotionally immature parents make it unsafe to be your authentic self as a child. As you manage your parents' moods, needs, and problems as a child, you learn how to abandon yourself from a young age in order to best survive the relationship. You had to accommodate your parents by becoming what they wanted or needed you to be. This means that at some point you had to tap out of your own inner world and disconnect from your intuition, and focus on other people's needs, feelings, and opinions instead. In his book *The Myth of Normal*, psychiatrist Gabor Maté explains that we are all born with a connection to our authentic selves, which allows us to know our own needs, communicate our boundaries, and trust our instincts. We are also born almost entirely helpless and therefore we have a strong need to attach to other humans for survival (namely our parents). Maté writes, 'We're born with a need for attachment and a need for authenticity; most people abandon their true selves (authenticity) to please others and keep the relationships (attachments), even if they are ones that are toxic and destructive.'[1]

If the environment and parental relationships we're born into require us to change ourselves in order to stay attached to our parents, then we will override our own needs, boundaries, and intuition to fit into the family system. We're hardwired to abandon our true nature to avoid being ignored, left, abandoned, or rejected. So if a child finds themselves with parents who can only accept them when they're polite, or agreeable, or achieve good grades, or look the way they want them to look, then it forces that child to disconnect from their true self, in order to maintain the attachment to that parent. Attachment will always trump authenticity for dependent infants and children because staying attached to our caregivers is literally life or death at this early stage of life.

Emotionally immature parenting requires you to cover up your authentic self temporarily, but who you are, at your core, cannot be erased. That is *you*. The you that has been there from the first moment of your life. That cannot be forever lost, but simply hidden, and the process of recovering from emotionally immature parenting is the recovery of that part of you. As we heal – be it in therapy, in nature, in relationship, in solitude, through books, or courses, or podcasts – we are essentially finding ways to be more of ourselves. Finding ways to accept our emotions instead of fighting them; finding ways to feel safe to say what we think instead of what other people want us to say; finding ways to have a loving, supportive relationship with ourselves. Personal development superstar Brené Brown says, 'Authenticity is the daily practice of letting go of who we think we're supposed to be and embracing who we are.'[2] Part of the process of becoming your authentic self is accepting and loving (and releasing) the past versions of yourself, and all the ways you coped with life after a childhood with emotionally immature parents. As you reflect on the coping strategies you've used so far in your life, and ask yourself whether they're still working for you or not, just know that the more you heal, and the more of your adapted self you shed, the more your authentic self will be revealed.

## COPING STRATEGIES

There are thousands of ways people learn to cope with life and the more awareness you have of your methods, the more choice you'll have in whether you continue on with the same strategies, or release what isn't working for you. For the rest of this chapter, we'll look in more detail at the common coping strategies of people-pleasing and self-abandonment, being hyper-independent, and avoiding or numbing your emotions, all of which are often adopted when children have to adapt to emotionally immature parents.

### The Need to Please

During secondary school, I would make my way home from school, run straight up to my room, and spend time drawing and listening to Celine Dion. My dad and sister would be home but we would be separate and the house would be quiet. At around 5 p.m., my mum would get home from work. My body would tense as soon as I heard her key in the door. She would announce herself, loudly: 'I'm home, hello, where is everyone?' I would immediately scan her tone of voice, trying to figure out what mood she was in. Was she annoyed, angry, or upset? Trying to predict her mood meant I might be able to adapt and become what she needed, be it someone who might cheer her up, soothe her, impress her, or just stay out of her way. *This is how I learned to be a chameleon*: someone who can change based on who they are with to please the other person and influence their mood. This ability started off as a way to manage my mother's moods, but became something I transferred onto my other relationships, and so three decades of people-pleasing began.

People-pleasing is a coping strategy unconsciously designed to manage other people's unpredictable moods and avoid their judgments of, or anger toward, you. If you spent your childhood walking on eggshells, it means that at some point you learnt that changing how you behave around your parents could impact how they treated you. What a superpower! As a helpless child faced with the task of coping with an unaware, powerful adult who was not able to control their emotional responses, you discovered a way to find some control. By being good, or nice, or polite, or helpful, or funny, or distracting, you found a way to secure (at least some of the time) your parents' approval. However, what starts as parent-pleasing often quickly turns into people-pleasing. People-pleasing is a smart coping strategy in many ways, helping us maintain connections and avoid feeling rejected, but it comes with a hefty cost to our sense of self. Each time you laugh at things you don't actually think are funny, or alter what you say so the person you are with will approve, or agree when you want to disagree, or say yes when you ought to say no, you're abandoning yourself. You're denying your authentic self a voice and a place in the world.

As children, we're often asked to abandon ourselves in order to be nice, or polite, or good; being made to feel silly for not wanting to sit on Santa's knee (aka a strange man in an odd costume), or being encouraged to hug your uncle who you saw only once in a blue moon, or being forced to share your toys before you'd learned how to share so your parents weren't embarrassed. These kinds of scenarios were fueled by parents who were people-pleasers themselves, and who found it hard to disappoint people. Having parents who were more concerned with how you behaved than how you felt would have sent you the message that what other people think is more important than how you feel. If, in those moments when your parents were faced with the choice of hurting someone else's feelings or overruling your boundaries as their child, your parents prioritized the other person, it would have sent you the message that your feelings don't matter.

Likewise, if your parents consistently put their feelings before yours and took up the majority of the emotional space in the home, or if they took their feelings of anger seriously but dismissed yours, or if they were more interested in being right than being kind to you, it means they prioritized their ego over your feelings, and you would likely have received the message that other people's feelings matter more than yours.

All of this leads to self-abandonment, and an identity built on being 'nice' and 'good' rather than authentic (because being your authentic self didn't work well with your parents). Self-abandonment is a coping strategy designed to avoid conflict, maintain relationships, and avoid being rejected – by overriding or suppressing your needs, feelings, and boundaries. It means ignoring your instincts, neglecting your needs, judging yourself, and suppressing your feelings.

Do you make sure everyone around you is OK before considering your needs? Do you find it hard to take care of yourself? Do you find yourself hitting a brick wall of burnout on a regular basis? Do you feel bad for saying no? All of this indicates that you were taught to ignore your own instincts, feelings, and boundaries at some point. That you learned to override yourself in deference to the feelings of others, and that you may unconsciously be operating from the belief that other people matter more than you.

If you had to abandon yourself to survive your relationship with a parent who needed you to fit in with them rather than making space for you, you may never have learned that people can dislike you, disapprove of you, be offended by you, or disagree with you – and you can still be OK and get on with your day. You may have never been taught that it's OK to disappoint people, and that it's a part of life and human relationships to get on with some people and not others. You may never have been shown that someone can be mad at you, and that you will be OK.

Here are some ways to stop abandoning yourself and to start advocating for yourself instead:

- Ask yourself regularly what you are feeling (and take your feelings seriously).
- Get used to asking yourself what you need (*see pages 128–132*) – and try to meet *your* needs as much as you can.
- Look after yourself as well as you look after other people.
- Stop being so nice.

Allow yourself to be a person who is sometimes good and sometimes not. We are all a bit of everything, and you do not need to be nice all the time. You are lovable and good enough whether you are nice or not. As Carl Jung said, 'I'd rather be whole than good.' Now is the time to be whole; to accept and embrace all of you: good and bad, nice and not nice, quiet and loud, ambitious and lazy, selfish and compassionate, thoughtful and inconsiderate. We are all a bit of everything, and it's time to give yourself permission to embrace it all, and to know that you are still worthy of love and connection regardless.

## Hyper-Independence

As soon as Laura came into my therapy room, I felt surplus to requirements. She oozed efficiency and seemed more grown up than I'll ever be. Her life was well organized, she was doing well in her career, loved her house, and was fit and healthy. However, she was lonely. She had a few reasonably good friends and a partner who she liked and who treated her well, but she still felt alone. Laura's mother was very critical of her when she was growing up and would scrutinize everything about her, from her outfits to her school grades, her hairstyle, and her piano-playing. Her father was absent a lot. He worked away for weeks at a time and when he returned, he was tired and tended to isolate himself from the family. She came from a 'live in separate rooms family' and would spend most of her time at home in her bedroom with the door shut. She grew up without a soft place to land. With no one safe to go to with her emotions, no one to go to and say, 'I need help with this.'

Laura recalled being a sensitive child who cried a lot, until she was around 10. This was when her parents separated and her mother's high standards intensified, and when Laura went to her in an emotional state her mother ridiculed or ignored her. She said she stopped crying or asking for much after that. She became self-sufficient, sensible, and grown up (at the age of 10) and she carried that efficiency and self-reliance with her into adulthood. Laura's hyper-independence made complete sense in response to her childhood, because when your attempts at emotional connection or requests for help are refused time and time again during childhood, especially by your parents, it seems sensible to adjust your expectations of people – to assume that no one else is available for connection or support either, and to become your own source of support instead. If you find it hard to ask for help even when you're overwhelmed, or if you take on a lot without delegating, or if you always want things done your way, or if other people being loving or caring feels a bit icky, it's likely that you got the message somewhere along the line that you're on your own and that you must act accordingly. Hyper-independence is a coping strategy unconsciously designed to protect us from being abandoned, and to reduce or eliminate the risk of feeling let down or helpless.

We are born with the desire to live in community, to be around others and be in relationship with other people in some form. As newborns we are born with one main skill: crying to draw the attention and care of other humans. Living alongside other people as part of a society is central to the human species and is part of how we survive; we are generally stronger and safer in a group than in isolation. So if you choose to do things all by yourself, over and over again, even when help is available, or if you find yourself in relationships with people who can't look after themselves and need you to take care of them, or if you find the implication that you can't cope offensive, it's because you learned that you are the only person you can truly rely on. Your hyper-independence makes sense, and I bet it's also been very useful in many ways, but I wonder also what you might be missing out on as a result?

Being very self-sufficient is a good idea when you are growing up without supportive parents. However, as Laura discovered, it also has its downsides. She had become so capable that she really didn't need anyone else, which made her romantic relationships feel pointless. She didn't share much of herself with her friends, leaving her feeling like they didn't really know her. She had a partner, but she didn't talk to her about anything significant or important, which made the relationship feel superficial. Independence is an important skill, but extreme self-sufficiency means you are missing out on the comfort of believing that someone will catch you when you fall (and denying yourself the benefit of testing the theory out now and then).

## Avoiding, Numbing, and Suppressing

Emotional experiences make us human. Emotions have been described as 'energy in motion,'[3] a natural passing through of energy that shifts us from one state to another, usually following an external trigger (for example, what someone says) or internal trigger (for example, our own thoughts). They are there to offer guidance and connection to the moment; however, the experience of some emotions can feel painful or overwhelming in our body, and we can spend a lifetime trying to avoid, numb, or suppress certain emotions. Have you ever found yourself in a conversation about something sad, but instead of feeling emotional, you feel nothing? You know you *should* be feeling something, but all you feel is numb and empty (and curious about whether other people ever feel like this, too). Have you ever had a stressful day and reached for a glass of wine to 'take the edge off'? Or found yourself 40 minutes into an ice-cream-and-biscuits marathon after a difficult day? Or realized that you've been scrolling on social media for an hour when you've got a big to-do list? These are some examples of how we avoid and numb, and are some of the ways you may have learned to cope with emotions that are too exhausting or overwhelming to feel.

Ideally, we learn how to tolerate, regulate, and manage our emotions in childhood because this is when we learn whether:

- our emotions are safe to feel
- we can cope with our feelings or not
- our feelings are acceptable to other people

We learn these things by having calm, emotionally regulated parents respond to our big and messy feelings as a baby and toddler, and by having them help us navigate emotions verbally as children to make them feel more manageable. As a 2022 public health paper found, 'Parents play a crucial role in how children develop emotion regulation, as well as influencing their child's temperament and neurobiological characteristics. When parents are sensitive and responsive to their child's emotional needs, the child learns to manage his or her emotions more and more effectively.'[14]

Numbing or avoiding emotions is a coping strategy that develops when a child learns that emotions are unsafe, overwhelming, or simply not welcome. Emotionally immature parents often leave you to deal with your feelings alone, without the comfort or guidance that you need as a child to help you process them in a healthy way. Over time, your brain adapts by muting those emotions altogether. You were wired to look to your parents for emotional validation. If, when you showed your sadness, frustration, or excitement, you were met with an irritated, dismissive, or indifferent response from your parent, you would have concluded something along the lines of: 'My emotions don't matter' or 'My emotions are a problem.' It also makes emotions feel scary; if you experienced big emotions on your own as a baby, toddler, or child, without the calming presence of a well-regulated adult, you would likely have felt completely overwhelmed and terrified. This fear of emotions stays with you and so it can feel as though you won't be able to cope with intense emotions as an adult. Dr. Jill Bolte Taylor, a neuroanatomist, studied the biochemical lifespan of an emotion, finding that it is roughly 90 seconds. Taylor says that when we fully experience an emotion, the physiological response that's triggered lasts about 90 seconds before it dissipates.[5] This tells us that, assuming that you allow yourself to feel your emotions and don't interrupt that process with avoidance or numbing, emotional responses don't actually last that long. However, if your experiences with your parents meant that you learnt to shut down your emotions as quickly as possible, it's likely that emotions feel never-ending, because you are never able to fully feel them and therefore conclude and exit your emotional experiences.

Here are some experiences that might have caused you to shut down your emotions as a child:

- **Your emotions were ignored or minimized.** If you cried, you were told to 'stop being dramatic.' If you were scared, you were called 'too sensitive' or told to 'toughen up.' After a while, your brain gets the message: 'Don't feel anything, because they don't love me when I do and it doesn't change anything.'
- **Expressing intense emotions led to punishment or guilt.** If showing anger, sadness, or excitement triggered a negative reaction from your parent, you would have learned to suppress your feelings and emotional reactions to avoid conflict.
- **Some emotions were OK and some were not.** If there were unspoken rules in your family about which emotions were OK and which were not, it would have sent confusing messages about how valid your feelings were. It may also have been the case that some emotions

were deemed OK for the females in the family (maybe sadness and anxiety) while others were deemed OK for the males (anger, for example).

- **You had to be the 'mature' one.** If your parent leaned on you emotionally, venting about their issues and expecting you to help them with their problems, you would have learned to detach from your own emotions, because there was no room for them.
- **Your parent was unpredictable or chaotic.** If you never knew how your parent would react, shutting down emotionally would have felt safest. A way to become invisible and avoid their unpredictable reactions.

These strategies don't just disappear once you grow up. Here are some of the ways this coping mechanism might show up in your life now:

- **You struggle to identify what you're feeling.** For example: You go through a stressful event (maybe falling out with your partner or having a health scare) but instead of feeling upset, you just feel nothing.
- **You feel emotionally disconnected in relationships.** For example: You feel neutral when your partner tells you they love you, without a feeling of warmth or connection.
- **You zone out or 'disappear' during stressful situations.** For example: You're in a heated argument and suddenly, it's like the sound turns down. You hear the other person talking, but you feel detached, like you're watching a movie rather than being in it. You feel blank.

- **You rely on distractions to avoid feeling anything.** For example: Scrolling endlessly on your phone, binge-watching TV, drinking, eating when you're not hungry, or staying so busy that you never have to sit with yourself.

Emotional avoidance isn't a flaw – it's a learned response that once served a purpose. But you deserve more than just 'getting through' life in a detached state. You deserve to feel your emotions and to be able to access the highs and lows of life fully and authentically. If you suppress feeling angry, sad, and disappointed, it's going to be hard to feel excited, joyful, or content, because you can't selectively numb emotions. Trying to avoid the 'bad' feelings means you block out the 'good' ones, too.

Here are some ways to start reconnecting with your emotions:

- Be curious about how you're feeling, even if you draw a blank at first. Name any feelings you do notice, even if they are vague. You can start small – if 'sad' feels too strong, maybe just go for 'off' or 'unsettled' instead – and build from there.
- Try to sit with emotional discomfort for a little bit longer. Remind yourself that emotions don't last long when you feel them. If you don't resist or block emotional energy, it will keep moving.
- Support yourself and your body while you are feeling difficult emotions. Practices like breathwork, dancing, stretching, humming, or walking can help you sit with your emotions for a bit longer.

Reconnecting with your emotions can take time and is something ideally done with the support of a therapist. It can seem like a big leap to feel your emotions if you've been used to avoiding them, so take your time. You will get there.

## THANK YOU AND GOODBYE

The ways you learned to navigate and survive stress, relationships, your own thoughts and emotions, and life in general makes complete sense based on the way you were raised and the things you experienced as a child. If you abandoned yourself in order to adapt to what other people wanted you to be, it's probably because it helped you feel safer in relationships. If you've spent years in toxic relationships despite trying to get out of them, maybe it's because you learned how to deal with toxic people, so it feels familiar. If you use alcohol to unwind every night, it's likely because alcohol creates a relaxed sensation in your body that you can't currently achieve in any other way. If you have been over-functioning and pushing yourself for decades, maybe it's because it's the only way you've known so far to block out the noisy thoughts in your head.

However, a useful question to ask yourself as you heal is: 'Is this working for me *now*?' Coping strategies that worked wonderfully at 18 might not hold up in the same way at 38. Equally, some of your methods of coping in life and in your relationships that have been around for a long time might still be working quite well. It's a question of how you want your life to feel, and what needs to be released (or retained) so that you can move toward that. In order to heal and let go of coping strategies that are no longer working for you, it's useful to give yourself grace for how you've coped so far, and to forgive yourself for the things you wish you had done differently. Your coping strategies developed for a reason, and they have been 100 percent effective so far in helping you to survive and continue on with life. As a child who didn't have parents to support, mentor, and guide you in the ways that you needed, you managed to generate effective ways to cope with life. You adapted. You did what was required. This is, in itself, incredible. Let's thank past you for being so resourceful, and recognize that future you can do things a bit differently.

■ ■ ■ ■

Forging a new path for yourself requires forging a new relationship with yourself, and next we're going to talk about how you can become your *own* reliable, good enough, emotionally mature parent.

# PART III
# HEALING

CHAPTER 8

# BECOMING YOUR OWN EMOTIONALLY MATURE PARENT

No matter what sort of childhood we had, or how our parental relationships unfolded, or whether or not we had the start in life that we needed, we must ultimately all become our own parent. We must at some stage and age find ways to structure our own day, feed ourselves, make big and small decisions, get some exercise, make money, manage our fears, make our bed, and find things to do in life that we enjoy. If, however, you had to do this before you were ready, or if you were prevented from learning how to understand your needs and care for yourself because of your parents' lack of attunement, it can make the process of becoming your own parent bumpy.

Typically, the way in which we parent ourselves, and the extent to which we do so, correlates with how we were parented ourselves. This is because we don't just experience our parents, we internalize their treatment of us (and their treatment of themselves a bit, too). Internalization is the 'process through which individuals integrate the values and standards of key persons, such as parents, into their own self-identity.'[1] Our self-identity informs how we treat ourselves and the quality of our self-parenting. If someone received parenting that generally met their needs and was supportive, loving, and somewhat predictable, it's likely that they will create a life as an adult that takes their needs into account, with a generally supportive and loving inner dialogue, and with a comforting structure that they've carved out for themselves. The reins of responsibility will at some point have been metaphorically and unconsciously handed over to them from their parents. However, if someone's parenting involved a lot of criticism and high expectations, with a focus on what they did and achieved rather than how they felt, it's likely that they will parent themselves harshly, perhaps creating a life filled with to-do lists, diets, long work hours, punishing exercise regimes, and little joy.

Learning how to parent yourself in a healthy way is one of the most pivotal points in any childhood healing journey, because it's when the script gets rewritten. When you get to look clearly at all the unhealthy, unconscious, and unspoken practices that helped your parents and ancestors survive, and say, 'Nope, that's not for me. I'm going to do things differently.' This is the point at which you consciously start to treat yourself better than your parents treated you. So, how do you go about parenting yourself well when you don't have that experience to internalize?

When I was pregnant with my daughter, I was working at an NHS mental health service in London and stumbled upon a rare gem of a supervisor, Joan. She had been a counselor for the best part of 40 years and was not only a trusted colleague and, I imagine, an excellent therapist, but also a very safe person (by safe, I mean someone who is generally conscious, aware, and present, rather than someone responding unconsciously from their unprocessed trauma). In the latter stages of pregnancy, I became quite obsessed with seeking out parenting advice. I was fascinated to learn how different people approached the task of raising children, and I was looking for ideas on how to parent in a healthy way in lieu of being able to use the parenting I received as inspiration. So I asked Joan, who had two grown-up children, to summarize the core of 'good enough' parenting in her opinion. She said that it requires two things that are of equal importance: love and boundaries. One without the other doesn't tend to end well, she said; a child who is loved but who has no guidance, structure, routine, or boundaries misses out on developing core life skills like self-discipline and delayed gratification (waiting for the good bits and accepting the not-so-fun bits). A child who has boundaries without love experiences life and people as cold, harsh, and unforgiving, and they don't get the chance to cultivate inner warmth, softness, and safety.

Love and boundaries. This is the foundation on which we can base emotionally mature parenting, and when translating this into a reference for self-parenting, it's useful to think about self-nurture and self-discipline. Becoming your own parent essentially means taking care of yourself, deeply, in all aspects of your life. Be it physically, emotionally, spiritually, financially, relationally, or otherwise. Shortly we'll break down the four core of pillars of self-parenting, but before that I want to tackle why it can be so hard to consistently parent ourselves well.

As you'll see soon, there is nothing particularly groundbreaking or profound about the basics of healthy self-parenting. I'm fairly certain you will be familiar with doing or trying to do all of it at some point during your adult life, and yet it can be so difficult to actually achieve. Doing the things that you know are good for you – eating well, getting enough sleep, saying no when you feel overwhelmed, going out for a run once in a while, getting a good dose of nature, drinking enough water, spending time doing things that you enjoy – these things can feel so out of reach much of the time. But why?

## WHY IS IT SO HARD?

Sometimes life makes it particularly difficult to take care of yourself and to parent yourself well. Circumstances that come to mind include when you are parenting young children, when your key resources (time and money) are very low, or when you are in an acute state of grief, loss, or sadness. In these instances, it can be tough (or nearly impossible) to do the things that you know are sensible and good for you – especially if you haven't inherited a good self-parenting structure from your own parents. Sometimes, though, even without any significant barriers in the way, it's still difficult to parent yourself in the way you want to. Cue a frustrating cycle of what feels like self-sabotage, followed by your best efforts to take care of yourself, followed by falling off the wagon again and beating yourself up.

One explanation for this is that perhaps you have been trying to look after yourself with a dysregulated nervous system all these years (we cover this in detail in the next chapter) and dysregulated nervous systems tend to crave quick comfort and familiar chaos. In the same way that trying to parent a child when you are constantly stressed, busy, and frazzled, with an overwhelmed nervous system, tends to lead to unmet needs and drama, so too with self-parenting. Another explanation is that trying to do what's good for you when you haven't healed from a childhood that damaged your self-worth is like trying to push treacle up a hill, and perhaps once you do enough work on yourself to *believe wholeheartedly* that you deserve the home-cooked food instead of the bag of crisps for dinner, or that you are worth getting a good night's sleep rather than saying yes to the extra glass of wine, or that the side hustle you've been working on matters and is deserving of your committed time, then self-parenting will become a whole lot easier.

There is, however, also something habitual about how we take care of ourselves (or neglect ourselves). Familiar behaviors that we automatically repeat, and that compound to either become nourishing habits or self-sabotaging patterns. Becoming more conscious of what you are doing, or not doing, to take care of yourself, and being intentional with how you self-parent, can overwrite old habits, and create new ones, more easily than you might think. A final thought on what can get in the way of taking care of yourself well is that we can get stuck in the perfectionism trap and think that we need to be making the right choices 100 percent of the time. As we discussed in Chapter 7, people can be very judgmental of some coping strategies, and when we do something because it's familiar or feels good (even if it might not be the most sensible option) it can bring with it a lot of shame. This shame can stretch a single week of imperfect choices into an entire month of self-sabotage.

In the same way as we only need our parents to be 'good enough,' we only need to be 'good enough' parents to ourselves. Self-parenting doesn't need to be perfect. Sometimes you can make decisions that are not sensible and still stay on track overall in terms of taking care of yourself. You can go to bed late a couple of days a week, and have too much chocolate, wine, or beer, or say yes when you should have said no, or skip your morning run in favor of some daytime TV… and still be OK. Do what you can and let go of the rest. There's always a chance for a do-over, and healing is a work in progress.

## THE FOUR PILLARS

Next, we'll look at the four core pillars of self-parenting:

1. Knowing What You Need
2. Nurture
3. Emotional Regulation
4. Gentle Discipline

As you read through them, try to view each area through the lens of love and boundaries. Never too harsh, but always with an awareness of self-responsibility. Used to support you, never to punish you. Nurture and self-discipline – because you deserve both.

### 1. Knowing What You Need

One of the many legacies of having emotionally immature parents is finding it hard to know what you need. This is often due to a combination of having to adjust to your parents' needs and suppress your own needs as a child, along with not being helped with your feelings as a child, leaving you disconnected from your own emotions. Questions like 'How are you feeling?' or 'How do you feel about that?' are common in emotionally healthy homes. This tends to get internalized by those children, leaving them more able to ask themselves how they feel and what they need as an adult. However, if you were rarely, or never, asked how you felt as a child, it makes sense that you don't automatically ask yourself that now. If no one checked in with you and took an interest in what you were experiencing internally, it's unlikely you would think to check in with yourself as you go about your day-to-day life. And without doing this, you are vulnerable to being disconnected from yourself and ignoring or bypassing your needs.

Checking in with yourself can be as simple as asking yourself: 'Have I drunk enough water?' or 'Do I need a snack?' It might also mean asking yourself why you found that conversation triggering, or what it was about your colleague's comment that left you wanting to cry in the bathroom. I think of this as taking your emotional temperature; checking in with where you are at emotionally. We need to do this quite often if we want to stay on top of our moods and keep some sense of balance.

## IDENTIFYING YOUR NEEDS

In order to start taking your emotional temperature, simply start asking yourself: 'What do I need? Is it...'

- solitude
- social contact

- activity
- relaxation
- nature
- space
- creativity
- play

Of course, sometimes you won't know what you need, and you might draw a blank with this part of self-parenting at first. However, the more you sit with curiosity and gently inquire with yourself about how you're doing, the clearer and more specific your answers will become. It's also useful to make sure you are living a life that has enough space in it for you to consider your needs. Just as a permanently rushing, busy parent often becomes too overwhelmed to check in with their children, we can mirror this process when self-parenting. If you find yourself often plowing through crammed days that leave you with little or no time to pause and reflect, it's going to be difficult to develop a dialogue with yourself about what you're feeling and what you need. So try to create some time and space where you can, and make some room for yourself in your life.

Once you develop a curious dialogue with yourself, then comes the consideration of how to meet your needs. It isn't always possible to meet your needs in real time – sometimes work schedules, school pick-ups, visiting in-laws, or looming deadlines get in the way. Nonetheless, the process of thinking about what you need and acknowledging your feelings is still important. It can also be possible to make small changes in order to meet your needs more of the time.

In the same way as a 'good enough' parent might make adjustments to give their child more of what they need at different times, you can do the same for yourself.

If you recognize a need for more social contact, consider how you could make this happen. If you feel the need to be more creative, could you find 20 minutes to draw, paint, bake, or build this week? Consider what helps you feel more relaxed – crosswords, reading, listening to music, etc. – and then try to find 15 minutes to do that toward the end of the day. Is there a part of you that longs to create and try something new? Can you get a set of watercolors and dedicate an hour on Saturday to painting your fruit bowl? Do you find yourself skipping meals and crashing at 4 p.m. because of it? If so, how can you make mealtimes more regular? It needn't be complicated, but you will need to take what your body and mind is craving seriously.

This checking-in, considering, and adjusting process is a core component of emotionally mature self-parenting. It is responsive care, and it's something that you may not have had much of as a child, so it may feel like quite a lot of effort at first; but remember that you are worth that effort. It will become more natural over time; the more you do it, and the more it becomes a habit, the easier it will become. You can also turn it into something practical. Write some of the prompts or questions above (and others that suit you) on Post-it notes and stick them around your house. Set reminders on your phone so that at the same time each day you are nudged to consider: 'How am I feeling and what do I need right now?' This will put you back in the driver's seat of your own well-being, and lay the foundations for the life-changing skill of healthy self-parenting.

## 2. Nurture

It is a key role of a parent to nurture their child, to 'care for and protect somebody... while they are growing and developing.'[2] It is of equal importance in self-parenting. Nurture involves cherishing, encouraging, looking after, and taking care of. When we stop nurturing ourselves, we stop growing, and when we're not growing, we're not really living. We can nourish ourselves physically (good food, movement, sleep) and emotionally (reading, creating, connecting with emotionally safe people). If you didn't have a consistently nurturing experience with your parents it might feel unnatural to nurture yourself as an adult, but luckily there are thousands of small, simple ways you can become more self-nurturing.

At the core of self-nurture is nourishment and comfort. A nourishing action or activity is anything that helps replenish you rather than deplete you; anything that gives you life, instead of taking it away. Nourishment can come in many forms. Nature has long been regarded as healing, and as naturalist and activist John Muir said, 'In every walk with nature one receives far more than he seeks.' Spending time in nature can nourish you back to a more vital, connected state. Eating good food is another act of nourishment. My first port of call when I'm feeling emotionally or energetically off is to think about the foods I've been feeding myself recently. To check in with myself about whether I'm eating 'real' foods or too many artificial, processed foods. Restoring more balance in that area is always my foundation for feeling better. Spirituality can also be fundamentally nourishing – seeking a connection to 'source.' Whether you call it source, God, higher power, universe, it's ultimately about a connection to something bigger than you that helps you access your wisdom, and puts into perspective those daily human anxieties and struggles. Whatever it is that nourishes you, do more of that. Sitting with a good book can be nourishing. Meeting with an old friend can be nourishing. Watching *Frasier* reruns can be nourishing (as I know from experience). Do it however and whenever you can. Everyone deserves to be nourished, and if you didn't get enough of it through loving contact as a child, you deserve to be nourished all the more as an adult.

Life is full of unforeseen problems, stress, worries, awkward conversations, anxiety-provoking work presentations, and unexpected bills. In order to manage the onslaught of issues that come with a full and active adult life, we need to find a buffer. Something to soften the hard bits. Without this we will quickly grind to a halt, be it through burnout, breakdown, or illness. This is why comfort is so important; seeking it, creating it, and making it a non-negotiable part of your life. Comfort is part of how we nurture ourselves, but it can seem like an optional (and even indulgent) perk of life, rather than something you need. However, if you want to heal and live a life that isn't dominated by struggle, then comfort is vital.

In the 1950s, American psychologist Harry Harlow conducted various experiments with baby monkeys. He set up two pretend mother monkeys: one made of wire with a bottle of milk attached to it, and the other, known as the 'cloth mother,' without milk. He wanted to gauge whether the baby monkeys would be more drawn to food or tactile comfort, and his findings concluded that tactile comfort was sought out much more strongly than food. The monkeys would drink the available milk but then return to the cloth mother for the rest of the day and treat it as their safe base, in spite of the fact it didn't offer milk.[3] This shows how basic and fundamental our need for comfort is from birth.

## LEARNING TO COMFORT YOURSELF

Regular comforting experiences are part of an emotionally healthy life, and also something we can lean into more in times of stress and hardship. When you're particularly in need of soothing, that's when it pays to know what comforts you and how you can create it in simple ways. If you didn't have a childhood that included much softness, gentleness, or comfort, or if you've simply forgotten to include it in your life as an adult, here are some ideas to help invite more comfort:

- Create a comfort corner or area in your home. Be it a chair, a room, or a small nook, make this space as cozy, relaxing, and soothing as possible. Blankets, cushions, candles, dim lighting, bright colors, patterns, neutrals, a rug, books. Whatever brings you comfort, bring it in.

- Make a specific list of things, activities, or places that soothe you: favorite songs, that purple blanket you love, trips to the movies, going swimming, old TV shows with no surprises, mint tea, the tapestry room in the V&A Museum in London, the sound of the ocean (in real life or through headphones). Refer to this list when you are in need of comfort, or make some of these things part of your daily schedule.

- Comfort can be external (soft blankets and tactile rugs), but it can also be internal (comforting thoughts and feelings). Consider what might bring you internal comfort, such as meditation or journaling, and do more of that when you can.

## 3. Emotional Regulation

Emotional regulation refers to the ability to feel your emotions, while simultaneously thinking about your reactions and responses to the situation. It's the experience of feeling *and* thinking. Allowing yourself full contact with your feelings, while still acting in a way that supports you, your well-being, relationships, and long-term goals. Being able to regulate your emotions means you feel your feelings rather than suppress them, but your reactions stay congruent with your wider self. Although adults can experience more than 220 unique emotions, Paul Ekman identified six primary emotions – biologically based feelings that appear early in the first year of life: joy, sadness, fear, anger, disgust, and surprise.[4] However, as babies we have not yet developed our frontal lobe, which is responsible for regulating these emotions. We rely entirely on our caregivers to regulate our emotions for us, by responding to our needs, offering comfort when needed, space when required, and loving contact when asked for. Through this process of regulation, which continues in different forms throughout childhood and adolescence, our frontal lobe grows and we learn how to regulate our own emotions.[5]

Being emotionally regulated as an adult doesn't mean staying endlessly calm or never getting angry; it's feeling the full spectrum of emotion but maintaining a connection to your rational self at the same time. It means you will usually be able to reassure yourself rather than need to find external reassurance. It means you will be able to feel angry, wronged, or offended and still maintain a connection with your rational thoughts and respond accordingly. This is what we learn through responsive parenting, and without that it can be difficult to regulate your emotions as an adult. If you didn't learn how to regulate your emotions during childhood, then now is the time to develop this life-changing skill.

## LEARNING EMOTIONAL REGULATION

Here are some ways to start developing emotional regulation skills:

- **Notice and identify.** Notice your emotions as they arise and label them: 'I'm feeling angry,' 'I'm feeling irritated,' 'I'm feeling so sad,' 'I'm feeling lost.' Notice what those emotions feel like for you, in your body. Become familiar with the sensations that emotions like anger, sadness, excitement, guilt, shame, joy, frustration, loneliness, and boredom create in your body – heavy shoulders, tingly skin, sore stomach, heaviness, a knot in your stomach, etc. – so that you can quickly recognize them.
- **Create a deliberate pause.** Try to pause between feeling and doing, or feeling and saying, or feeling and reacting. This

pause will give you space to regulate (bring your rational mind on board) rather than just act from your emotions automatically. This pause is where powerful change happens.

- **Soothe while you wait.** Emotional regulation is not about skipping past your emotions, or blocking them, or speeding them up. It's more a case of waiting for them to pass through you without acting too strongly. You can support yourself while this happens by using your list of comforting things, activities, or places from the previous section (*see pages 134–135*).

- **Express and communicate.** Experiment with expressing your emotions in a way that fosters connection, rather than escalates conflict. This is not always easy, but try different ways of communicating how you feel when you need to. This can be greatly helped by number 2 (the deliberate pause).

- **Perspective and recovery.** This is where emotional resilience is built. You may not need to do this often (perhaps for more significant emotional events rather than day to day) but where there is opportunity to reflect, try to make sense of any triggers and be curious about your emotional responses.

## 4. Gentle Discipline

The final pillar of self-parenting is gentle discipline. This means knowing what practices are good for you and doing them often, and avoiding practices that aren't good for you as much as you can. It can also involve giving yourself a structure. Structure can bring great comfort; a way to contain our human impulses, busy brains, and endless distractions.

Having a general structure to your day or week also lets you know what to expect. In the same way as parents offering their children a nighttime routine, at roughly the same time each day, allows their bodies to relax and prepare for sleep, so too do the routines we provide for ourselves as adults. This requires discipline, though, because life is full of things that are much more fun than having regular mealtimes, going to bed at a sensible time, and going for an evening walk. Gentle discipline involves honoring your commitments and requires some level of focus, persistence, and self-control. This is a really important component of self-parenting, but it must be done with love and compassion for yourself and your humanness. You can't be disciplined all the time, and you don't need to be, but trying to stick to a structure that helps keep your life functioning well is part of looking after yourself. A loving parent helps their child show up for the gymnastics classes that they asked to go to, brush their teeth twice a day, and drink enough water – even when they're not in the mood for any of it.

There is no shortage of advice out there on how to achieve your goals, build better habits, and improve your life with more discipline. However, much of this advice, despite how motivational it may be at first glance, doesn't take into account the challenges faced by those who grew up with parents who were actively critical when they got something wrong, or shaming when they tried something new, or disinterested in their wins, or negative about their potential. This creates a whole new layer to wade through when trying to be disciplined. Nevertheless, having some structure and commitment around activities that are good for you is something you deserve, so let's figure out how to make it happen.

## COMMITTING TO YOURSELF

You don't need to do it all. You do, however, deserve to take care of yourself well – while resisting the urge to do it perfectly and 100 percent of the time, or not at all. Focus on one area of discipline at any given time, and let that be enough. Below are some ideas for gentle self-discipline. There's a variety of activity types, because where you might be currently with these practices can vary at different times in your life. You can use the activities below as inspiration (or pick your own) but the important thing is to **choose one** activity to focus on over the next couple of weeks.

- Get more sleep.
- Move more.
- Spend some time working on a personal project each day.
- Cook for yourself more.
- Shower daily.
- Go to your GP about the issue you need to get checked.
- Do nothing for 15 minutes a day.
- Journal three times a week.
- Commit to no screens for 60 minutes before bed.

- Create a 10-minute morning ritual – you can use one of the following suggestions or one of your own:
  - ~ Sit with a drink and write down three intentions for your day.
  - ~ Stretch for 10 minutes.
  - ~ Wash and massage your face.
  - ~ Read a chapter from a grounding or inspiring book.

Hopefully this chapter has given you some ideas or reminders of ways to look after yourself more deeply and lovingly. It's difficult to stick with healthy self-parenting skills if you're living with a nervous system that's on high alert, though. The nervous system is king when it comes to either having a good quality of life or existing in perpetual struggle, and it's a powerful part of any childhood healing journey. So buckle up and get ready to learn how to build a resilient, healthy nervous system in the next chapter.

# CHAPTER 9

# PEACE AND SAFETY

As soon as we leave the womb, we are thrust into a world of uncertainty. The loss of the warmth, safety, and constant supply of nutrition that we get *in utero* is, in many ways, the most profound loss of them all. From then on, we have to find ways to get our needs met and to secure safety in the world. We start collecting data from day one – data about how safe the world is, how available people are, how different behaviors create different responses in other people. This data is stored in your nervous system. The state of your nervous system dictates the quality of your life. Regardless of the other details of your life – financial status, where you live, what job you have, what you look like – ultimately, if your nervous system is dysregulated (i.e. you feel stressed, worried, tense, overwhelmed, reactive, or frozen), none of it will bring joy. On the other hand, if your life doesn't seem to be full of the things people often strive for, but you feel generally at peace and at ease, you've won the golden prize. One of the best gifts of a well-regulated nervous system is that it allows you to feel satisfied. It means you don't have to live in a perpetual state of longing for more, wanting something different, wanting to be something else, or somewhere better. It allows you to accept and embrace what is, rather than what could be.

The central nervous system is a network of neurons running from the base of the brain down the length of your body that sends messages all over your body to keep things functioning and to keep you safe. It plays a part in most aspects of how the body functions, from your physical health and immune system to how emotional you are and the types of thoughts you have. The nervous system moves into different states depending on how threatened or safe you're feeling. One state is commonly referred to as 'rest and digest.' This is when your nervous system – and you – are in a mode of neutrality or relaxation. When everything is pretty much OK. When you perhaps feel calm and generally grounded. In this state, your body can recover, heal, and digest (food, emotions, experiences, interactions).

The other state is fight-or-flight, the reactive, high-alert, protective part of your nervous system. It responds to threat – whether real or perceived – and focuses on keeping you alive and safe. If you experienced parenting that left you feeling generally safe, you are likely to have a flexible nervous system, and be able to move between the two states with ease. If, however, you grew up feeling on edge, unseen, misunderstood, overwhelmed, or frightened, it would have created an unregulated nervous system, leaving you feeling uncertain and unsafe much of the time. While worrying, being busy, and rushing can be a sign of a dysregulated nervous system, so too can being in 'freeze' mode. 'Freeze' is the lesser-known third state, which goes with the fight-or-flight state. It's another available response for a nervous system that feels under threat. In everyday life, the freeze response can look like: feeling so overwhelmed by your to-do list that you end up doing nothing; spending hours zoned out on the sofa; endless scrolling on your phone; or putting off dealing with something stressful.

Without safety, we can't have peace. We can't feel settled. It's difficult to find our way back to ourselves when life throws us off course. This is one of the reasons so many people feel anxious, depressed, and generally terrible despite having a good life. When you feel awful for 'no reason,' chances are you are operating from a dysregulated nervous system and living in a state of tension. Life lived without a general sense that everything will be OK is a life of almost-constant worry. Spending your childhood in fight-or-flight mode can also mean that you become very used to feeling unsafe, to the point that unsafe people or situations might be given the thumbs-up by your nervous system because that feeling of not being safe is familiar. This can keep you stuck in cycles of toxic relationships, decisions that don't turn out well, and finding yourself in environments that hurt you.

## HOW CHILDHOOD SHAPES THE NERVOUS SYSTEM

So how does the nervous system develop in childhood? We learn largely through our parents whether life and the world are basically safe or not. The thing with emotionally immature parents is that they're still struggling to feel safe in the world themselves. They were still trying to figure out how to cope with their big emotions and difficult thoughts while trying to raise you. They were still trying to learn how to keep their anxieties and fears at bay while you needed them to help you with yours. And so, if your father was one person at home and another when out in public, maybe angry at home and charming outside the house, or your mother was disinterested at home but social with everyone else, this will have sent you the message that people are fundamentally inconsistent and untrustworthy. Or if your parents were not able to manage their anxiety about you hurting yourself, and each time you fell over they panicked or screamed or cried, you'll likely have got the message that the world isn't safe and that you can't cope with difficult experiences. If, whenever you were upset or hurt and went to your parents for comfort, you were met with irritation instead of empathy, it will have wired your brain to think that the world is harsh and that people are uncaring.

Part of the complex system of nerves that makes up the nervous system are mirror neurons. They're like a bridge between your inner world and other people, and they help you develop in important areas such as empathy, social understanding, and emotional connection. Mirror neurons develop when someone (ideally a parent) sits with you and engages closely with you as a baby, infant, and young child. When a parent is frequently attuned to you and what you're trying to communicate as a child, you experience a sense of mirroring and bonding. A parent being attuned to their child really means that they can meet their child where they are at in that moment. They can tune in to what might be happening for their child internally, and adjust what they do and say in response. Being able to attune to a child requires the parent's nervous system to be in a somewhat regulated state, because a dysregulated adult is more concerned with their worries and problems and the practical parts of life than with playing peekaboo (a great game for mirroring!) with a six-month-old baby. Your nervous system developed in relation to your parents' nervous systems and in response to the quality of engagement they were able to offer you.

This is why nervous system healing work is an important part of recovering from a childhood with emotionally immature parents, because your nervous system developed in response to your parents, who were struggling to manage their own nervous systems. All the experiences you had as a child affected your amygdala, your brain's alarm center. The amygdala is the part of your brain that picks up on threat and danger. It's very sensitive in childhood and is constantly gathering information about your environment, and storing it to use in the future to keep you safe. If you grew up around a lot of stress because your parents couldn't effectively manage their nervous systems, it would have fed your amygdala the message that the world is unsafe and full of threat.

Not having the safety net of parents who could manage their emotions and make space for what was happening *for you* disrupts your internal alarm system. As a result, your adult years may be filled with anxieties about many things, if not everything, because your alarm system (amygdala) will be highly sensitive. This means that feeling calm is probably not easy or common for you. We are born with a threat system which keeps us alive, but during infancy and childhood a different part of our brain grows: the prefrontal cortex. This part of the brain helps us manage our fear-based reactions and add some logic, so that anxiety doesn't take over. It's what helps us stop worrying and start problem-solving, the part of our brain that calms us down. 'The human brain is characterized by the significant expansion of... the prefrontal cortex. This expansion is thought to underlie... the capacity to engage in high-level strategies to regulate anxiety.'[1] Early childhood (up to around age five) is when the prefrontal cortex forms most significantly, although there is also a period of sensitivity and growth in adolescence as well. The prefrontal cortex develops most rapidly in early childhood, but continues to form until the age of 26.[2]

So, how does it grow? In response to attuned care from your parents. Every time your mother picked you up and fed you when you cried for milk as a baby, or reacted calmly to your spills as a toddler, or talked to you about your friendship troubles in primary school, or watched you play your favorite sport as a teenager, it grew your prefrontal cortex and contributed to your experience of safety and connection in this world. Each time your father rocked you to sleep as a baby, or asked you where it hurt when you fell over as a toddler, or helped you with the homework you were worrying about as a child, or asked how you were feeling about your exams as a teenager, it was building that part of your brain that would help you feel content and at peace in your 40s, 50s, and 60s. We draw on our childhood experiences of feeling safe with our parents and internalize that feeling, so that we then have that sense of safety within us and can independently feel safe as adults.

If, however, your cries as a baby were met with little or no response, or your spills and trips made your parents shout, or your difficulties with your friends and school work weren't recognized, or your parents wanted to control you during your teenage years rather than understand you, then your prefrontal cortex would not have developed fully. If you were surrounded by arguing parents while your brain was developing, or had to navigate a parent chronically misunderstanding you, punishing you, criticizing or ridiculing you, being manipulative, or denying your reality, you would have become used to feeling unsafe with people (and in the world in general). The ways your parents acted, reacted, and interacted with you would have deeply affected your developing brain and nervous system.

So, how can those of us who didn't have enough experiences of feeling emotionally safe as a child develop a flexible nervous system? A nervous system that is able to experience either end of the emotional spectrum and find its way back to a steady baseline. To feel joy and excitement *and* safeness and boredom. To be able to feel fear, and also be able to feel hopeful. For this, we need to start living a nervous-system-friendly life. Spending childhood in a mild to severe state of tension tends to mean we unconsciously create a life of mild to severe chaos. Too busy, lots of rushing, or numbing with TV, social media, food, alcohol, instead of resting. Nervous system health is the route to experiencing life as a grounded person who feels generally safe in themselves (and safe to be themselves).

These are the core pillars of a nervous-system-friendly life:

1. Boundaries
2. Movement and Stillness
3. Play and Pleasure

## 1. Boundaries

There are few things that overwhelm the nervous system more than walking through life without setting boundaries. Boundaries protect your peace. We are constantly in an energetic exchange with other people, and our nervous systems are busy collecting information from other people (and their nervous systems). This process is called co-regulation and it describes the interplay between each of us. It's why being around other people who are stressed can make you feel stressed, and being around people who are calm can help you feel more grounded. This happens organically and a 2023 study states: 'Not all aspects of our abilities to share experiences and exhibit synchronous behaviors in interactions are necessarily conscious. Some co-regulation processes unfold slowly or occur quickly without comprehension.'[3] The nervous systems you put your nervous system near to will make a big difference to how regulated you feel. It matters who you spend your time with. This doesn't mean you should disregard your relationships with people who are often in fight-or-flight mode or who struggle to stay steady, but it does mean that part of healing involves noticing the impact different people have on you, and making adjustments.

### GETTING BETTER AT BOUNDARIES

Notice how you feel after you've spent time with each of your friends, family members, or colleagues.

- Who throws you off-center and leaves you feeling foggy and tense?
- Who helps you feel calm and grounded?

- How can you find ways to spend more time with people who benefit your energy and nervous system?
- Could life feel better if you limited your time with those who leave you feeling drained or frazzled?

Relationships are a constant energy exchange; choose who you exchange your energy with wisely.

In the process of healing and building a life with stronger foundations, the boundaries you set with your parents become increasingly important. True healing involves reconnecting with yourself – understanding your needs, learning how you wish to be treated, and cultivating deeper love and respect for who you are. As this unfolds, you will develop a lower tolerance for being treated badly. Unfortunately, your parent(s) may not be on the same journey, and their behavior may continue to cross lines you can no longer ignore. If one or both of your parents are still in your life, you may begin to question what level of contact feels truly supportive to your well-being. In recent years, the concepts of going 'low contact' or 'no contact' with parents have entered more mainstream conversations, both online and in therapy rooms.

Opting for low contact with your parent(s) can be a powerful way of protecting yourself when the relationship becomes more draining than supportive. This might mean reducing how often you see or speak to them, or choosing specific forms of communication that are more manageable for you; for example, texting or emailing instead of calling. Low contact is a good option when other attempts at setting boundaries with your parent have been unsuccessful, and when you recognise a need for space and distance for your own emotional well-being.

Choosing to go no contact is a bigger step. For those who have a generally positive relationship with their parent(s), or for those who carry a strong sense of guilt and obligation, even imagining this choice can feel unforgivable. It's still a decision that is unfairly shamed and misunderstood in society. No one wants to find themselves caught between protecting their well-being and maintaining a bond with their parents. And no one chooses to end contact with their parents lightly. It usually comes after decades of ignored boundaries, countless failed attempts at connection, and many moments of feeling hurt by your parents' words or actions.

Severing contact with a parent (or any family member) is a painful and often lonely decision. It is, effectively, leaving your tribe and even if your tribe is toxic or harmful, leaving it is alarming for your nervous system. Even if you have a partner, children, strong friendships, or an otherwise good life, losing contact with your parents often awakens a deep sense of loss and abandonment. Yet sometimes, it is the only way to preserve your mental health, self-esteem, and energy.

Some parents are simply too damaging to remain close to. Abuse, constant boundary crossing, or feeling emotionally unsafe should be taken as seriously in a parent–child relationship as it would be in a marriage or friendship. If a spouse repeatedly insulted you, dismissed your needs, and left you feeling insecure and rejected, very few people would tell you to 'Just put up with it.' The same applies to parents. Just because they are your mother or father, it does not mean that you should feel obliged to put up with, or excuse, harmful behavior.

If you are facing the painful choice of going no contact, I want to offer these reminders for moments of doubt or grief:

- You are choosing yourself, your growth, and your healing – and you should be deeply proud of that.
- You are not failing as a son or daughter by setting limits; you are protecting the child inside you who has already endured enough.
- Love and loyalty should never require you to tolerate mistreatment.
- Distance is a valid form of protection.

While no contact may feel lonely at times, it can also create space for deeper, healthier, and more nurturing connections to blossom in your life.

Boundaries aren't limited to relationships. Our boundaries buffer us from *all* external influences: the news, social media, work, socializing. As we talked about in Chapter 6 in the people-pleasing section (*see pages 107–111*), it can be difficult to set boundaries with other people after a childhood of not being allowed to set them. However, you are worthy and capable of experiencing the temporary discomfort of saying no to someone in order to create a life that doesn't overwhelm your nervous system. In her book *Daring Greatly*, Brené Brown says, 'So I bought a silver ring that I spin while silently repeating, "Choose discomfort over resentment." [This] reminds me that

I'm making a choice that's necessary for my well-being, even if it's uncomfortable.'[4]

Creating parameters for yourself that make life feel more manageable is a core part of self-love. How you spend your time is how you spend your life. Be intentional about what you fill your time with (especially your spare time outside of non-negotiable duties). What matters most to you? What brings you the most joy, peace, or meaning? As for so many of us, this might mean saying 'no' more often and cutting down on commitments. Kate Northrup writes, 'When you do less, you have more energy, time, and enthusiasm for the things that matter the most to you... When you do less, it doesn't mean you do nothing. You simply do less – but more of what matters.'[5] This includes spending time with people who you truly want to spend time with. Exercising choice around who you arrange to meet up with. This is all part of living a nervous-system-friendly life and healing from a childhood in which your nervous system was set to high alert too often.

We have never had so many ways in which we are being taken away from the present moment than we do right now in the world. Attention is the new commodity and there are many ways in which social media companies, brands, and advertisers try to get our attention and keep us looking at our phone or laptop, but this isn't going to keep your nervous system happy. Looking at screens for an extended length of time interferes with sleep, focus, and nervous-system regulation. Dr. Victoria Dunckley, an integrative psychiatrist and screen-time consultant, has discussed how excessive screen time can affect the nervous system. She writes that interacting with screens shifts the nervous system into fight-or-flight mode, leading to dysregulation – an inability to modulate one's mood, attention, or level of arousal in a manner appropriate to one's environment.[6] Setting limits around how much social media you use, or how much world news you will engage with, in itself sends settling signals to your nervous system that *you* are in control and that you will not be taken over by external influences.

Smartphones are one of the biggest threats to our nervous systems in the modern world. We were never meant to have access to so much information so much of the time and being exposed to so many people, thoughts, opinions, and ideas triggers our nervous systems to move into fight-or-flight. Historically, humans have lived in small, close-knit communities, typically ranging from 50 to 150 individuals.[7] In these small communities, we were only aware of local events and issues directly affecting our social group. In contrast, today we are exposed to vast amounts of information and the details of tragedies happening all over the world. This constant influx of global information is unprecedented in human history and requires boundaries to avoid this saturation of news and information causing nervous system issues. This is true for everyone, of any age; however, it's especially important to get a grip on screen use if you are someone whose nervous system developed alongside dysregulated nervous systems, rather than in the context of people who had well-regulated nervous systems (who were generally able to manage their emotions and respond rather than react). Creating a physical boundary between you and your phone (leave it in another room, only use it at certain times) is a powerful boundary-setting technique. As is choosing one day a week to be more-or-less phone or social media free, or limiting screen time to certain hours of the day. None of this is easy, but it's worth giving it a good shot.

## 2. Movement and Stillness

The nervous system likes balance. Too much of anything tends to stress it and tip us into fight, flight, or freeze mode. Some rest and some movement. Some stillness and some action. Moving your body, be it half an hour of walking, jogging, yoga, stretching, swimming, or anything else that takes your fancy, is great for your nervous system. It's been researched extensively and we know that 'repeating a physical exercise… stimulates the development of the prefrontal cortex, responsible for decision-making and emotional self-regulation. Thus, exercises not only improve physical performance but also contribute to managing stress and anxiety.'[8] Movement is a basic human need and in the words of Dr. Andreo Spina: 'Force is the language of cells and movement is what we say.' Throughout most of human history, our ancestors led nomadic lifestyles as hunter-gatherers, constantly moving to forage for food and resources. This required regular physical activity, such as walking, running, climbing, and carrying, which was integral to their daily survival. Human bodies are designed for regular movement.

Movement in nature is a double whammy that sends your nervous system all sorts of lovely, calming signals, encouraging it further into 'rest and digest' mode. So, if the choice is available, running on a path by a field or lake is likely to be more supportive for your nervous system than running by a road. And it's not just the scenery that's beneficial: 'A virtual reality forest including sound was found to improve stress recovery more than the same forest without sound, implying that the sympathetic nervous system shows increased recovery with nature sounds.'[9] Add to that doing a type of movement that you genuinely enjoy, and just 30 minutes can settle your nervous system considerably, giving your body space to fight off illness and select less worrisome thoughts and more present, focused ones.

So much can also be gained from stillness. Simply being. Not folding the laundry, or working on your project, or watching TV, or chatting to your friend. Not doing anything at all. Just being still and noticing where you are and what's around you. Noticing how your body is feeling and listening to the birds, or traffic, or people, or silence outside. This is inherently settling for the nervous system – once you get used to it.

## FINDING STILLNESS

It may take some time and practice for your mind and body to get on board with not being busy or occupied, and if this is a challenging activity for you, start small.

- Create a ritual around stillness if you can. Try spending 5 minutes at the beginning of each day, or during your lunch break, or just before bed, in which you just sit. In which you are simply still.
- Be curious about how your nervous system interprets the lack of doing – does it feel boring, strange, pointless?
- Keep going with it and build up the time or frequency as best you can.

Inviting stillness into your life is something your nervous system will greatly thank you for (once it's on board!).

## 3. Play and Pleasure

Play is a healing powerhouse. As play researcher Brian Sutton-Smith says, 'The opposite of play… is not work, it is depression.'[10] But so often we lose touch with the power of play as an adult. A study on adult play asked its 837 participants what they considered play and playfulness to be, and concluded that play is being in 'a flow state… It's invoking our inner child, the young self, that is innocent, joyful, magical.'[11] This sums up why living a life that is playful, or that includes play, can be a tough ask when childhood wasn't all that magical or joyful. It can be hard for those of us who had emotionally immature parenting to instinctively play or seek pleasure. Play is instinctive and a natural part of childhood, but if your parents were critical, harsh, easily angry, or disinterested, it may have shut down your natural playfulness. If your attempts at having fun, or being silly or playful, were shamed or squashed, time and time again, you would have learned that pleasure is not a positive thing. Sometimes the reason we unconsciously avoid play is because we have a difficulty tolerating pleasure.

In order to play, children and adults need to feel safe and secure, otherwise the essential practice of playing gets deprioritized. When childhood has felt more heavy than joyful, it often takes deliberate effort, patience, and healing to get to a place of playfulness as an adult.

So, what does it mean to 'play' as an adult? I like to think of this as doing something 'just because.' Just because you want to, just because it's fun. With no element of productivity, meaning, or purpose. It also includes being fun and playful. Silly, funny, light. Without these types of moments sprinkled into your days and weeks, life becomes heavy. Our nervous system becomes rigid instead of flexible. Life seems to be entirely serious, and while there are many things about life that are serious, and sometimes we must acknowledge those things, it takes its toll to live in that zone all the time.

Our productivity-obsessed society often reinforces the messages you may have got as a child about pleasure being something that should be earned or limited. Throw in certain religions – whether in the foreground or background when you were growing up – that suggest human pleasures are sinful, and it makes the perfect storm for finding it difficult to allow yourself to enjoy much about life or experience pleasure. Pleasure is part of healing and creating a peaceful life for yourself, not only because it creates a buffer for the inevitable difficult and stressful parts of life, but also because it connects us to the present moment. It's difficult to take pleasure in something while also being distracted.

## CREATING SPACE FOR PLAY

There are certain things we can do to deliberately try to bring more pleasure into our lives, but pleasure can be easily found in the everyday, too:

- Eating delicious foods and deliberately savoring the flavors and textures.
- Listening to music that brings you comfort, whether in an elevating or nurturing way.
- Finding warmth with cozy blankets, sunshine on the skin, or a hot shower.
- Touch and physical affection, in the form of hugs, massages, holding hands, or petting an animal.
- Being in a comfortable environment: your home, a soft bed, or an inviting chair.
- Being open to spontaneous joy and unplanned fun.

There is so much pleasure to be found in the everyday. Of course, life cannot be entirely about play and pleasure, but you deserve at least some of it to be. You are worthy of peace and safety, fun, and meaning. This is not always a one-person job, though. Your nervous system health is a significant piece of the well-being pie, but so too are your relationships. It's hard to live a full, satisfying, and meaningful life in isolation. We are social creatures, made for connection with other people from day one. However, being able to enjoy relationships, rather than experience them as threatening, painful, or constantly disappointing, is easier said than done after a childhood with emotionally immature parents. So, let's take a closer look at how you can start to love peacefully rather than painfully.

# CHAPTER 10

# LEARNING TO LOVE IN PEACE

The quality of your relationships directly affects the quality of your life. In her book *Daring Greatly*, Brené Brown says, 'Connection is why we're here; we are hardwired to connect with others, it is what gives purpose and meaning to our lives.'[1] However, sometimes our childhood overrides the desire for connection, and wires us for protection instead. If you consistently felt emotionally unsafe, misunderstood, overlooked, judged, physically unsafe, or unloved around your parents when you were a child, it contaminates how you experience other people and relationships. We use the data from our relationships with our parents to create a blueprint, so that we know what to expect from other people going forward.

## ATTACHMENT THEORY

Psychoanalyst John Bowlby developed a theory known as attachment theory, based on the understanding that our early experiences with our attachment figures (typically our parents) form the foundation for our emotional health as adults, and contribute heavily to our understanding of ourselves and the role of relationships. We develop internal working models based on our relationships with our parents, which go on to inform our adult relationships.

There are four commonly accepted styles of attachment that form in response to your relationship with your parents, influenced by how they responded to you, managed your emotions, interacted with you, and loved you. These are the four main adult attachment styles and the key traits that come from them in adulthood:[2]

## 1. Secure Attachment

### *Core Belief*

'I am worthy of love, and others are reliable and trustworthy.'

### *Traits*

- comfortable with intimacy and independence
- trusting and open in relationships
- good at communicating needs and emotions
- able to depend on others and be depended upon
- emotionally available and responsive
- handles conflict well and tends to have stable relationships

## 2. Avoidant (Dismissive) Attachment

### *Core Belief*

'I can only rely on myself; closeness is uncomfortable.'

### *Traits*

- values independence over closeness
- emotionally distant or aloof
- may avoid intimacy or commitment
- tends to suppress emotions
- pulls away when relationships get too close
- may come off as self-reliant but struggles with vulnerability

## 3. Anxious (Preoccupied) Attachment

### *Core Belief*

'I need others to feel complete, but I fear they will leave me.'

### *Traits*

- craves closeness but fears abandonment or rejection
- often needs constant reassurance
- emotionally intense and sensitive
- may become clingy or overly dependent
- worries about the partner's feelings or availability
- struggles with trust and tends to overanalyze behavior

## 4. Disorganized (Fearful-Avoidant) Attachment

### *Core Belief*

'I want love, but I fear getting hurt.'

### *Traits*

- desires closeness but fears intimacy and rejection
- can be unpredictable in relationships – hot and cold
- often has unresolved trauma or negative past experiences
- struggles with trust and emotional regulation
- may sabotage relationships or feel unworthy of love
- high levels of anxiety and avoidance mixed together

The quality of our attachment to our parents deeply affects the quality of our relationships in our adult lives. However, it's possible to shift your attachment style as you get older and to improve your relationships; research confirms that attachment isn't fixed, but can change over time. There's a concept in psychology called 'earned secure attachment,' according to which people who developed insecure, anxious, or avoidant attachment styles as children can become more securely attached as adults.[3] A 2011 study found that earned security often develops when you connect with alternative secure, emotionally healthy people (friends, partners, mentors) as an adult – people who provide consistent emotional attunement and healthy connections.[4] Earned secure attachment also develops through internal reflection and healing work relating to trust, boundaries, and emotional intimacy. This is great news! Finding, creating, and prioritizing healthy adult relationships can effectively overwrite much of the damage done to your understanding of relationships by your parents.

## BUILDING BETTER RELATIONSHIPS

Relationships are an ongoing exchange of energy and there's much that can be done to shift the nature of the energy between two people. The rest of this chapter is dedicated to you learning how to have and enjoy healthier relationships, with greater trust, balance, communication, and authenticity. You deserve to associate love with peace, not pain. The following sections are written with romantic relationships in mind, but the principles can be applied to all relationships. There are many things outside your control in relationships (namely everything the other person does, says, thinks, and feels!) but here are some things that you can do to make your experience of relationships feel safer and more satisfying.

### Trust

When my first child was about 11 weeks old, I met up with an old friend whom I saw rarely but liked a lot. I was deep in the trenches of early motherhood, with sore, exhausted eyes, a constantly aching back, and a complete detachment from my normal functioning brain. She didn't dive straight in to holding my daughter Aphra; instead, she just watched the two of us for a while and then said, 'Look at that, she trusts you completely.' In that moment I realized what that look was that had been staring at me from the pram and the carrier and across the bed at 2 a.m. in the morning. My friend was right – it was the look of complete trust. We all come into the world fully trusting our parents, because our entire life and survival depends on them. We come into the world fully dependent on our caregivers, and particularly lined up to connect with our mother (although fathers matter immensely too, of course). This trust is an important part of the fabric that connects us to not only our parents, but to people in general. It is what allows us to communicate our needs as babies, have tantrums as toddlers, and run to our parents with bloody knees after we've fallen as four-year-olds, without fear of being rejected. When a parent responds to these moments with kindness it supports the child's belief that they can trust people, which is what contributes to that child growing up to have close friendships, and an emotionally intimate relationship with their romantic partner(s).

If, however, your moments of vulnerability as a child were dismissed, ignored, shamed, or criticized, it is likely that your trust in your parents (and people as a whole) would have been eroded each time. Emotionally immature parents tend to break the trust of their children – by letting them down time and again, or by brushing aside their emotional experience, or judging rather than supporting, or using the withdrawal of love and attention as a punishment. It's difficult not to assume the worst from people after you've experienced the worst from those who should have treated you the best. Our parents are our first loves, and although they automatically have our trust when the relationship begins, that trust can be eroded. This makes trusting our partners or friends complex, and yet we are repeatedly told that 'trust is the most important part of a relationship.' This is easier said than done after having your trust broken by your parents as a child.

Trust is best built gradually, and it's my belief that full and unconditional trust is not necessarily healthy. However, it's useful to try to get to the point at which your difficulty trusting doesn't consume or negatively affect your relationships. For instance, being preoccupied with what your partner may be doing when you are not with them, or being hypervigilant to what they say to you because you're on the lookout for verbal attack, make for an exhausting relationship.

## FINDING TRUST

Learning to trust people is in many ways a process of learning to give people the benefit of the doubt. This is no small task when you were let down by your parents in childhood. Here are a couple of ideas to help you start building toward being more trusting of other people. If you are currently in a relationship, consider trying one or both of them over a week-long period, and notice how this feels and what the impact is on the relationship, if any:

### Notice What They Are Doing Right

If your trust was broken by your parents, it's likely that over the years, you'll unconsciously have gone looking for evidence to back up your belief that people will let you down. In order to build a new belief (the belief that it's safe to have faith in someone) you will need to make a point of collecting evidence to support the new belief instead. Make a conscious mental note (or write down on your phone or in a dedicated notepad) when your partner does what they said they were going to do, or when they are consistent in their behavior, or when they are emotionally available and supportive, or when they admit a mistake, take responsibility, or communicate openly.

### Tell Your Partner What They Can Do to Help You Feel More Secure

This comes with the caveat that your partner is not obliged to follow through on doing everything that might help you feel secure; however, part of deepening trust involves deepening communication. Sharing what impact some of your partner's behaviors have on you can help the relationship grow toward a place of reciprocity and a dynamic that is unique to the two of you.

## Balance

Emotionally healthy parenting involves striking a balance between connection with and separation from your child. Closeness without merging. Relating without combining. This balance is important in all loving relationships; they all require giving part of yourself while retaining part of yourself. Productive love isn't boundaryless and all-consuming, and it also isn't shut down and distant. If you didn't experience this type of balance in your relationship with your parents, you might find yourself struggling to achieve it in your relationships as an adult. Perhaps you get lost in relationships and quickly lose your sense of self. Or maybe you resist sharing important parts of you and find yourself feeling at an emotional distance even in your closest connections.

When the balance between connection and autonomy isn't reached in a parent-child dynamic, it can create enmeshment. A parent and child can be enmeshed, and so too can an entire family. Family enmeshment is a pattern of overly close, overly involved relationships in which personal boundaries are blurred or even absent. In enmeshed families, members may struggle to develop a clear sense of individuality because emotional needs, responsibilities, and identities are entangled. There is an emphasis on being the same, adapting to make other family members happy, and prioritizing the good of the group, even if it's to your detriment as an individual.

Growing up in an enmeshed family or parental dynamic often leads to codependency as an adult: a dynamic in which each person expects their needs to be taken care of by the other person, or where one partner feels responsible for the emotional well-being of the other. This is connection without healthy boundaries and it can create dynamics that keep you entangled, suppressed, and depleted. It also creates a pattern of trying to manage other people (and of being managed by them): managing their moods, emotions, reactions, and behaviors, often in an attempt to save them from the difficult parts of life. One of the most damaging false myths peddled about romantic relationships is that it is your job to make your partner happy. It's actually impossible to make another person happy – happiness is, in almost every way, an inside job. However, often we create dynamics that are built on the requirement to make our partner happy, or we wait for them to make us happy, causing layer upon layer of disappointment and resentment. Imbalanced, codependent relationships often form from two people bonded by an inability to meet their own needs, having never been shown how to as a child.

The best way to start changing this kind of dynamic is by taking radical responsibility for meeting your own needs first and foremost. This involves being autonomous, checking in with your emotions, managing your moods, finding comfort when you feel distressed, taking responsibility for your day, resting, eating well, moving when you need to (*see pages 128–132*). In other words, parenting yourself and being completely responsible for your own well-being. This will free up energy and space in your relationships to enjoy each other. Connecting, instead of relentlessly problem-solving for one another. Laughing, instead of fighting. Living alongside, rather than living within, each other.

## Words

*'The single biggest problem in communication is the illusion that it has taken place.'*
George Bernard Shaw

It is a sad reality that emotionally immature parents are often not that invested in trying to understand their children. They are typically too preoccupied with their own stress, problems, or events of their day to pause and take a moment to make sense of what you are trying to say. You may therefore have had the repeated experience of talking (about insignificant things and big issues) and being misunderstood. This can leave you with the belief that you can't communicate well, or that the way you describe things and express yourself doesn't make sense. This often becomes echoed in your adult relationships: a frustrating feeling of being incompetent and unable to communicate your feelings or get your point across. 'Does that make sense?' becomes your mantra and it can lead to you shutting down in difficult moments for fear of being misunderstood (again). The problem was never you, though; the problem was that you had a parent who wasn't that interested in making sense of what you were saying, during the years when you were learning how to communicate. It's also true that if you had a very dominant, angry, or aggressive parent, you likely got the message that trying to communicate is pointless, after many experiences where negotiation, discussion, or joint resolution was not an option. This can further block your willingness to talk or listen in relationships, because you haven't had much of either experience as a child.

However, we are told, on repeat, that good communication is the foundation of a healthy relationship. That being able to express yourself clearly to your partner, and listen to them with open ears and an open heart, is the route to harmony in relationships. There is a lot of truth to this, but it doesn't take into account how deeply your ability to use and hear words is affected by spending your childhood communicating with emotionally immature people. Having a conversation with someone who is unaware of themselves and their own trauma, hurt, confusion, or fear, and who doesn't have the capacity to manage their emotions, is like being sucked into a nonsensical vortex. Up is down, left is right, and nothing quite makes sense. Words get constantly twisted and misunderstood, and it's often impossible to move through the conversation in a logical way.

This is especially true when the conversation is rooted in conflict or disagreement. Disagreeing with an emotionally immature parent quickly becomes a confusing battle. The usual rules of boundaries and conversations don't apply. If you know what it means to question yourself and your understanding of reality because your parents' words turned everything upside down whenever they got angry or upset, then you'll probably know that achieving 'healthy communication' in your relationships now is not as straightforward as it seems.

Not only does the way in which your parents communicated with you as a child matter, but the way they communicated with *each other* also plays a role. Children are always listening. Even when they seem to be absorbed in play, or are laughing, or daydreaming, they are still, at some level, listening. It's also true that they often pick up on more than words, and that they often tune in to the energy between the two most important adults in their lives, and make interpretations. If your parents' communication with each other was often toxic or disrespectful, or if you were caught in the middle of their conflicts, or had shouting and screaming as the soundtrack in your childhood home, it will have affected your understanding of how to communicate in relationships. So, too, would having parents who barely interacted with one another, or who didn't seem interested in connecting. Our experiences in childhood tend to lead to either repetition or avoidance; so, if you were the child of warring parents, it's possible that you either followed suit and have relationships that are full of conflict, or that you've gone in the opposite direction and avoid conflict at all costs – even when it's necessary. And if your parents were disconnected from one another, you might find yourself needy of reassurance in your relationships now, or avoidant of emotional intimacy.

## YOUR FAMILY COMMUNICATION STYLE

When you think about how communication was in your family when you were growing up, here are some questions you can ask yourself:

- What was the energy generally like between your parents?
- How did they communicate with one another?
- Was their relationship largely filled with harmony or conflict? Connection or disinterest?

It's likely to have been different at different times, but consider what you remember most about how they were when they were together.

Although it is generally unpleasant to have parents who argue a lot of the time, it's also not necessary to have parents who are constantly loving and harmonious, and living in a conflict-avoidant home can rob you of developing the skills to manage difficult issues and have tough conversations. Dr. John Gottman has written about the importance of 'rupture and repair' in healthy relationships, stating that when relational ruptures (conflict and arguments) occur between parents, the subsequent repair process is crucial for children involved.[5] By actively engaging in repair – saying sorry, talking calmly and rationally after the argument, coming to a resolution – parents show their children that restoring connections after disagreements is possible. It also shows them that difficult interactions don't have to mean the end of the relationship – which contributes to them developing a sense of security and trust in the robustness of human connection.

If, however, you were exposed to your parents' arguments and hostility toward one another without seeing many instances of them repairing, it alters how you come to understand what it means to communicate with someone you care about. It overrides the limits and boundaries that naturally occur in healthy relationships, such as not wanting to hurt your partner, or of being more invested in peace and reconciliation than in being right. If you were exposed to a lot of your parents' arguments, you may have learnt that relationships are an emotional (and sometimes physical) battleground; that part of connecting with someone means defending yourself, being right, and winning, rather than coming together and working through difficulties.

So, how to make the shift toward words that help rather than words that hurt? It's important to know that disagreeing and arguing can be useful in relationships. Some situations call for anger, and a relationship that survives mainly because one or both of you are heavily suppressing your feelings can only go so far. However, if you *often* find yourself in the verbal arena with your partner, battling, defending, and shouting, it's useful to make some moves toward more moments of harmony. Equally, if you avoid conflict at all costs and find yourself dismissing your partner's complaints, or avoiding saying anything that might cause an issue, then you might also benefit from the following ideas.

### *Say What You Need, Not What's Wrong*

The assumption that your partner knows what you're needing, feeling, and thinking is a cause of so many issues in relationships. It's easy to assume that telling your partner 'I'm tired' is the same as saying, 'I want to leave the party now.' Or that saying, 'Lucy was really hard work today' is the same as saying, 'I need a break from parenting duties for a few hours so that I can regain some energy.' Saying what you need and being as specific about it as you're able to be can go a long way toward making your relationships smoother.

### *Be Curious About Where They Are Coming from*

In 1978, David Premack and Guy Woodruff introduced the concept of 'theory of mind.'[6] It described, among other things, the process of recognizing that other people have different thoughts, feelings, and beliefs to you, and that we are all approaching each situation from a different perspective. It's easy to forget this though, especially with people we've known for a long time. We lose sight of the fact that our partner is not experiencing things in the same way as us, and vice versa. Doing your best to come back into a state of curiosity about what your partner might be thinking, feeling, or experiencing can reduce conflict and make your relationships a more empathic, gentle place to be.

## Showing Up

Surviving a childhood with emotionally immature parents can require you to hide yourself in plain sight. To hide your needs, thoughts, opinions, and personality. If there was little room for you and your emotions in your relationship with your parents, and if their ego and issues took center stage, you may have got used to shrinking into the background, or being quiet, or trying to make yourself invisible. Passive-aggressive parents can also create so much confusion that you are left with little choice but to hide yourself. If your mother said she was fine but looked furious, or acted like she was cross but said she wasn't, that's hard for a child to make sense of. Childhood is when we are learning what emotions are and how to read our own and other people's. If you had to cope with a passive-aggressive parent, you may have learned to shrink yourself down to avoid their anger, disappointment, or confusing responses. This strategy of hiding yourself was a smart way to manage the relationship, but it may have also become part of how you function in your relationships now.

You might find yourself in relationships with people without *really* being there. Going months, years, even decades without showing yourself to the other person. Avoiding being vulnerable. Letting them take up all the space. Being a fraction of yourself, all the time. This means that not only do your friends and partners never get the chance to know you, but you don't experience being truly known. Without allowing people to see you, you can never feel seen. Making yourself invisible in relationships is at the root of loneliness – the type of loneliness that can be felt even when you have friends and are married, or have plenty of people around you. Loneliness is a form of silent grief, an ongoing sense that someone or something is missing. Becoming more visible in your relationships will deepen your connection to people, which helps loneliness fade away.

So, how do you do this after a childhood of necessary hiding? After a childhood in which you were shamed or punished or rejected when you expressed your feelings and shared your true self?

It means learning to be yourself more of the time, with more people, rather than hiding. You don't have to share every thought and feeling with your partner or friends, but you can *consciously* choose to *share yourself and show yourself* enough to feel heard and seen. Start to slowly take the risk of being more visible by making yourself and your needs part of your relationships. Start small and with people who feel emotionally safe and healthy. This needn't be big, loud declarations or an outpouring of emotion (although it can be and that's fine, too). It could mean disagreeing, rather than automatically agreeing, or voicing what you want to do on the weekend, rather than only considering what your friend or partner wants to do. It's saying when something hurts your feelings, or giving your opinion when it feels important to do so. It's saying when you need a break or some rest or some alone time; letting your needs be known and being a part of the dynamic. Taking the leap of faith and letting yourself be seen by other people is something you deserve to do for yourself. Having authentic relationships is one of the most meaningful experiences you can have as a human: to let someone see you and love you, in your fullness. It's also only fair to share yourself with the world, because *the world needs you* and your perfectly imperfect, human, authentic self.

## PARENTING

In a book about emotionally immature parenting, in a chapter about relationships, it seems remiss not to talk about parenting your own children. Your relationship with your own child is one of the most significant and life-altering connections you can have, not just as a person, but as someone who is healing their own childhood wounds. Becoming a parent offers so much opportunity to learn and reflect, be triggered, make mistakes, and do better, and all of the progress we make and setbacks we experience with our own children are also felt by our own inner child in one way or another. There is a lot of opportunity for reparenting yourself within the process of being a parent.

If you've been reading these pages not only through the lens of your childhood, but also with your own children and parenting in mind, you will likely have picked up various things *not* to do if you want to avoid repeating the cycle of emotionally immature parenting. However, we haven't yet covered what *to* do in much detail. There are enough parenting books out there to keep you busily reading for the rest of your life, books on gentle, conscious, or emotionally aware parenting that go into detail about how to raise emotionally resilient and healthy children, and I'm not going to pretend that a few paragraphs can do this topic justice. However, there are some core foundations of emotionally mature parenting that are worth mentioning because, ultimately, parenting in an emotionally mature way as much of the time as you can is a good route to a healthy, enjoyable, and secure relationship with your child – and in that scenario, everyone wins. None of the following points need to be achieved 100 percent of the time, but striving toward them as often as you can is a good place to aim for.

## FOUNDATIONS OF EMOTIONALLY MATURE PARENTING

### 1. Emotional Regulation

- Managing your own feelings and stress, and being able to react to your children's behavior calmly rather than impulsively.
- Taking responsibility for yourself and managing your moods and needs effectively.
- Being accountable for yourself, apologizing when needed, and not being defensive or blaming.

### 2. Self-Awareness

- Being aware of how your upbringing is influencing your parenting, and having an awareness of your own childhood issues, triggers, wounds, and beliefs.
- Being open to self-reflection and growth.

### 3. Empathy and Attunement

- Tuning in to your child's emotional needs and experiences, and validating their feelings rather than dismissing or minimizing them. This will help you to see behavior as communication, not just as something to fix or control.
- Encouraging your child to experience his or her full range of emotions, and to express those emotions.

### 4. Secure Boundaries

- Providing structure and guidance without rigidity or authoritarian control. This involves encouraging autonomy while still keeping developmentally appropriate limits.
- Recognizing your child as a separate person with their own needs, personality, and pace.

Ultimately, the more you are able to approach parenting with an understanding that your child is their own person, and that, no matter their age, people deserve respect, love, and clear communication, the better the relationship will become.

It may be that you find yourself in the thick of your parenting journey and know that it's unfolding in a way that you are not proud of or happy with, and you may be worried that you can't course correct at this point. Every parent that has ever existed has had times when they were emotionally immature with their children. For those who haven't, I'm going to bet that they didn't spend much time with their children (and prolonged parental absence is a form of emotional immaturity, because it disregards the child's primary need for parental connection). Whether it's triggered by exhaustion, stress, financial pressures, relationship issues, ill health, or just the relentlessness of being responsible for another human, all present parents have moments of emotional immaturity. This doesn't mean that irrevocable damage has been done, or that it's too late, or that you've messed it all up. It's never too late to improve your relationship with your children, or to improve your mental health – which will benefit them in every way. The only point at which all hope is lost is when you give up working on yourself, and when you stop trying to deepen the relationship with your child.

Children tend to respond remarkably well when their parents change in a positive way. They are ready and waiting to connect more deeply with you (despite what they may say). Remember that the human brain continues to develop until the age of 26 (*see page 146*). Every patient, aware, open, and nurturing interaction between a parent and child until that age will improve their long-term mental and emotional well-being. And every patient, aware, open, and nurturing interaction after that age will still help life feel better and softer for them. Keep trying and keep healing.

If you find yourself with grown-up children and are filled with guilt and regret about how you were, or how things are with your children now, it's a painful and difficult place to be. It's heartbreaking to have growing awareness that you wish you'd had access to years ago when your children were small, when things could have been steered in a different direction. The fact that you've picked this book up (and have kept reading) shows that you want to work on yourself, and it may be that your current personal healing journey helps to improve your relationship with your adult children now. If your relationship with them has come to an end, however, let the things you wish were different become part of what you grieve. Wishing the past was different is a loss. A loss of how it might have been. A loss of what you hoped for. Let yourself grieve it all, and once you have grieved, carry forward only what's useful.

■ ■ ■ ■

I hope the ideas in this chapter contribute to you having more connected, safe, enjoyable relationships. There is, of course, only so much you can ever do to change a relationship on your own; the dynamics between two people are a strong force, and while you can make a huge difference, it's undeniable that change will happen more easily and effectively when you are both trying to move toward the same end goals. That being said, you can't make someone change. If you find yourself stuck in a relationship that feels painful, but worth continuing, accessing couples therapy is a brilliant resource, if you are able to.

Ultimately, I hope that you have more moments in which you feel peaceful and relaxed when loving someone or being loved. I hope that you have fewer moments of feeling abandoned or rejected or forgotten by others, and that you find good ways to cope when you do. Connecting with other people is complicated and difficult when your most important and first connections in the world were not smooth, but the truth remains that *you deserve* decent, healthy, loving relationships. This includes having a good relationship with yourself, but after facing the painful parts of your childhood, releasing old beliefs, questioning how things have been, and choosing new ways of coping, it can be difficult to know who you are anymore. Healing is, in part, a process of re-forming your understanding of yourself, so let's take some time to consider who is left after shedding so much of your past self.

# CHAPTER 11

# WHO AM I NOW?

Healing from childhood trauma means releasing layers of pain, defense mechanisms, and old beliefs that may have shaped your sense of self for a long time. Discovering who you truly are afterward can be both freeing and challenging. It means learning who you are beyond the version of you that you had to become during your childhood. It involves becoming yourself, rather than unconsciously living out who you had to become, or who you were told you were. Although this sounds like a big task, it's more a process of removing from your life as many of the things that stop you being yourself as you can, and doing what you can to support reconnection to yourself. The rest will take care of itself.

## A LIFE ROOTED IN SAFETY RATHER THAN SURVIVAL

A childhood with emotionally immature parents is a childhood spent surviving rather than relaxing. If one or both of your parents were not able to manage themselves and their emotions, it means you had no choice but to be on high alert. Connecting with yourself more deeply as an adult is supported by consciously creating a life based on safety. This is part of reclaiming those childhood years spent in survival mode, and making your adult life different. Because your nervous system got used to scanning for danger, and being hypervigilant and on high alert, creating a life rooted in safety now will have to be a conscious and intentional process. It's worth mentioning, though, that safety doesn't mean avoidance. Avoiding things that challenge us, or that feel difficult in some emotional, physical, or spiritual way, gives the *illusion* of safety. Systematic avoidance is ultimately the act of building your own prison. True safety is found in allowing yourself to feel all your emotions without telling yourself that you're being over the top. It's found in practices that replenish you and that activate the 'rest and digest' part of your nervous system, rather than the fight-or-flight part. And it's found in feeling safe to explore life; to try new hobbies, start projects, change careers, travel, take up ballet dancing at 50 years old, or start painting, running, or baking. When you feel safe to try and explore, you have reached a new level of security.

Unwavering safety also means that you're not in a rush to define yourself. Often we attach to the ideas we have of ourselves in order to feel safe and valid. Sometimes these beliefs and definitions are protective in some ways: 'I'm a good person,' 'I'm helpful,' 'I'm thoughtful'; but even positive self-definitions can keep us trapped and unable to be our full and authentic selves. We can also define ourselves negatively, or tell ourselves stories that keep us stuck and make us inflexible.

## THE STORIES WE TELL OURSELVES

We don't come into the world knowing who we are. Our parents, first and foremost, tell us who we are through their actions and words and interactions with us as children. All the moments you experienced with your parents would have given you information about who you are and how you should be in order to get your needs met. This would have contributed to you unconsciously developing stories about yourself. Stories that made the world feel more predictable. Stories that turned into rules for living.[1] When parents are stuck in their own trauma it makes it impossible for them to see their children accurately, and so a lot of the data those children collect is skewed and distorted. This means that some of the stories you've been telling yourself about who you are might not be entirely accurate. Your self-concept is not permanent, though – you *can* change how you think and feel about yourself.

Below are some common stories, beliefs, and self-definitions that often form after being parented without emotional awareness. There are many more that you might have developed, but you may resonate with some of these, or they may help you to identify yours:

## 'I Have to Earn Love by Being Useful or Successful.'

### *How It Forms*

If love and attention were only given when you achieved something (e.g. doing well at school, helping around the house), you may have formed the belief that your worth depends on your productivity or usefulness.

### *Impact*

You might be prone to overworking and struggle to relax, as well as feeling unworthy unless you are constantly doing or achieving something.

## 'I Am Responsible for Other People's Emotions.'

### *How It Forms*

If your parent was emotionally needy or unstable and you had to manage their moods, this may have led to the belief that you must fix or regulate other people's emotions.

### *Impact*

This can lead to codependent relationships (*see pages 166–168*), excessive guilt, and exhaustion from taking on emotional burdens (that are not yours to carry).

## 'Being Happy or Successful Will Make Others Resent Me.'

### *How It Forms*

If your parent was jealous, dismissive, or downplayed your achievements and joys (e.g. 'Good for you, it must be nice to have it so easy'), you may have learned that success or happiness leads to rejection and guilt.

### *Impact*

You might self-sabotage, downplay your achievements, or feel guilty for experiencing something good when others are struggling.

## 'If I'm Not Struggling, I'm Not Trying Hard Enough.'

### *How It Forms*

If love and praise only came when you were enduring hardship or 'pushing through,' you may have grown to associate struggling with worthiness.

### *Impact*

This can lead to chronic overworking, burnout, and difficulty enjoying life when things are going well. You might also subconsciously create struggle where it isn't necessary, and find it hard to enjoy your successes.

## 'If I Fully Relax, Something Bad Will Happen.'

### *How It Forms*

If you grew up with an unpredictable or chaotic parent, where moments of calm were often disrupted and followed by sudden conflict, emotional outbursts, or crises, you might have come to unconsciously associate relaxation with vulnerability or impending danger.

### *Impact*

This can lead to chronic hypervigilance, difficulty resting or switching off, and a need to stay busy or anxious to 'stay ahead' of potential problems. Even in safe situations, you might feel uneasy when things are going too well.

These are stories. They are not facts. They are not truths. They are not permanent structures by which you must live your life forever (although they can feel like it). You are in many ways undefinable, as all humans are. Naturally, human beings fluctuate; we shift and change, and are different in different situations and relationships. It can be challenging to detach from the ideas you've held about yourself for so long, but here's an exercise that can help you start to rewrite the stories you've been telling yourself for all these years:

## REWRITING YOUR STORIES

### Step 1: Name the story

- Ask yourself: 'What do I believe about myself at the deepest level when I feel rejected, unseen, or unworthy?'
- Write down 1–3 beliefs about yourself that were likely shaped by your early environment. Here are some examples:
  - ~ 'I'm not lovable unless I'm useful.'
  - ~ 'I'm too much.'

- ~ 'If I need support, I'll be abandoned.'
- ~ 'I have to stay small to stay safe.'

## Step 2: Deconstruct the Inheritance

- For each belief, explore its **origin** and impact:
  - ~ Where did I first learn this belief?
  - ~ Whose voice does this sound like?
  - ~ What has it cost me to carry this?
- Write freely. Let the emotions come. You are safely naming the pattern, not judging yourself for it.

## Step 3: Rewrite the story

- Consider:
  - ~ What is actually true about me that this belief ignores or distorts?
  - ~ What would you say to a child who held this belief about themselves?
  - ~ How would I see myself if I had never been taught this?
- Then write a **direct, assertive response** to the old belief:

  For example: 'That's not true. I am not too much – I was surrounded by people who couldn't meet me where I was. My emotions are valid. My needs matter.'

## Step 4: Confirm this alternative story

- Turn the truth into a personal powerful statement – something clear, embodied, and strong. This is your **reclaimed identity**. Here are some examples:
  - ~ 'I am worthy of love even when I'm not giving.'
  - ~ 'My emotions are wise and deserve space.'
  - ~ 'I no longer betray myself to keep the peace.'
  - ~ 'I belong, just as I am.'
- Say it aloud. Repeat it slowly. Write it on paper or a Post-it note and put it where you'll see it daily.

## Step 5: Integration

- To anchor this shift, take one small action this week that reflects your new belief.
  - ~ What would someone who believed this truth do differently today?
  - ~ What boundary, decision, or act of care aligns with this new truth?

Something that can make it difficult to detach, or separate, from the way we've come to define ourselves is the belief that we are trying to change our fundamental personality. If you have been told since the age of four that you're lazy, you probably started to believe it early on, and somewhere along the way that belief may have started to feel like it's who you are; an innate part of your personality. If, however, those same traits (daydreamy, slow to follow instruction, in need of a lot of downtime) had been interpreted as being creative, for example, and that's the label you'd been given since the age of four, it would be likely that being creative would have become 'part of your personality' instead.

## THAT'S JUST MY PERSONALITY

We are not born with a formed sense of 'self.' We develop our understanding of who we are through our experiences, mainly in childhood. The concept of the 'self' and personality has been considered, debated, and written about extensively for decades. Humanistic psychologist Carl Rogers offered a theory of personality, saying it's related to the development of our self-concept: who and how we consider ourselves to be. He identified two core elements: the ideal self and the real self. The ideal self represents who you want to be – the traits you aspire to have and the person you would like to become. The ideal self is typically the product of parenting and society. The real self is who you really are – your authentic self, the version of you that exists without excessive external pressures or judgments. The real self is dynamic and responsive to real-life experiences. Rogers emphasized the importance of these two 'selves' being somewhat aligned, or at least not too different to one another, in order to feel psychologically well. He said that it's the gap between your real self and your ideal self that causes suffering. Childhood trauma can distort the real self by causing you to develop negative self-beliefs such as 'I am not good enough' or 'I am not worthy of love,' and in order to cope with these beliefs you may then construct an ideal self that is unrealistic, one related to what you think might earn you love and acceptance, taking you further and further away from your real self.[2]

The fields of evolutionary psychology and genetics also tell us that we are not born as blank slates and that we enter the world with certain inherited traits, making us more likely to have a preference for certain tastes and flavors, to being highly sensitive, or prone to addiction issues. Epigenetics tells us, however, that our environment also plays a major role in what gets amplified and what doesn't. If someone is very sociable and extroverted, there will be a component of that behavior that they were born with (probably an ability to tolerate a lot of stimulation, or perhaps a need for it). But there may also be an aspect of their social behavior that comes from their childhood: perhaps needing to be loud or bold in order to be heard in their family, a desire to keep up with extrovert parents or siblings, or a need to be seen by their parents. Also, it's likely that this person would be told and would come to believe that being very sociable is their 'personality.'

Sometimes, what we think of as our personality is actually a collection of traits and behaviors that we've developed to manage our childhood environment. This can mean adapting the way you are, what you feel, and your needs in order to fit in. It can also mean adapting to the roles you were assigned, subtly or clearly, in your family when you were growing up: the quiet one, the sensible one, the helpful one, the screwup, the sporty one, the clever one. We take to heart who we are told we are by our parents and siblings, and hold on tight to these identities. Over time we become those things (or think we do).

This can be a helpful way to survive in emotionally unaware families, but as adults it becomes restrictive and we end up unconsciously denying parts of ourselves to maintain our role as the quiet or sensible or clever or funny one. It blocks us from exploring who we really are.

Emotionally immature parenting – and the criticism, blame, control, and manipulation that goes with it – doesn't change who you fundamentally are, but it can temporarily distort it. As you heal and start to restore a sense of safety, self-worth, and belonging, and rediscover your voice and connect with your emotions, your authentic self will naturally emerge. Some of the traits and ways of being that you developed in your childhood will likely stick around too, and that's OK. They have worked so far in helping you to survive, and some of them will likely have now become 'who you are.' Just know that you always have the right to change, adapt, and release. You don't need to define yourself too rigidly. Nature is always evolving, changing, shifting, and growing – and you, my dear, are part of nature.

## FINDING YOUR PURPOSE

Life is inherently uncontrollable and mysterious, and we have little available to us to help us feel like we have some agency over our own lives. We are, after all, hurtling through space on a ball of rock, alongside around 8 billion other people, some of whom have a very different agenda to us, and so I understand why subscribing to the concept of finding your life purpose is appealing. I have also noticed that this seems to be of particular importance to those of us who had to manage more than we should have as children. Perhaps feeling fundamentally out of control as a child deepens the desire for control as an adult. British philosopher Alan Watts reminds us of something basic and profound in his lecture 'Mysticism and Morality': 'The meaning of being alive is just being alive... It's so plain, so obvious, and so simple. And yet here is everybody rushing around in a great panic as if it were necessary to achieve something beyond all that.'[3]

There's nothing wrong with identifying your life's purpose and building your life around it. However, there's also nothing wrong with having no idea whatsoever what your purpose in life might be. It can be enough to look after yourself well, do work that is meaningful to you, nurture your relationships, enjoy the natural world, and be present as life unfolds, until you reach the end of your time. It is enough simply to live. There is, perhaps, no need for a grand purpose, but an emotionally unsteady childhood tends to make us forget this option because it pulls us away from the present moment and takes us further away from ourselves by forcing us into hypervigilance too soon. Having a stressful childhood often sets our inner thermostat to stressed, and so our adult life becomes lived in the same way: feeling like we are behind, failing, and running out of time. This is your reminder that you do not have to prove your worth with grand achievements, or by having a big impact. You are enough as you are.

## CREATE A LIFE THAT SUPPORTS CONNECTION WITH SELF

As you venture further toward your authentic self, and further away from the person you had to become to manage your childhood, it is useful to create a life that supports self-connection. There are so many aspects of modern life that make it difficult to connect with yourself: from the vacuum that is our smartphone, to the lure of social media, long work hours, disconnection from the natural world, other people's expectations, the quest for more, the list of things we should be doing in order to live to a hundred, and so on. Much of this blocks our ability to hear ourselves, or to tune in to our intuition and self-trust. When healing from emotionally immature parenting, it's important to make self-connection a priority, and there are ways to create a life that protects and promotes self-connection:

## Create Rituals

Here are some ideas:

- a 20-minute morning stretch
- 10 minutes spent lovingly making and enjoying your morning matcha
- listening to music on your commute
- lighting a candle while having your afternoon tea
- an evening breathwork practice
- before going to sleep, placing one hand on your body and naming 1–3 things your body did for you today

Any of these small touchpoints can become part of the rhythm of your life, and they will all help you stay in connection with yourself.

## Curate Your Environment

- Be mindful of what you fill your home or space with.
- Designate one area to yourself if you can. Fill it with colors, textures, and items that you love.
- Make your space a reflection of you so that you feel more deeply grounded when you are in it.

## Find Time

Resist the temptation to fill every hour of your day. There are some seasons of life that require a full schedule, but there's usually a way to dial it back, even just slightly, so that you leave yourself with some time that isn't assigned to anything. It's hard to connect with yourself if you're constantly doing something.

## Take Your Emotional Temperature

If you don't have a curious relationship with yourself, it's not easy to connect with yourself, in the same way as you're unlikely to be invested in a conversation with someone who asks zero questions, or who seems to have no interest in you. We can only cultivate a good relationship with ourselves if we're curious about what's happening for us. Ask yourself regularly what you're feeling and what you need.

■ ■ ■ ■

We are all a beautiful work in progress. Self-discovery after healing is more about ongoing curiosity than knowing, with certainty, who you are. I would say that it's never a good idea to try to reach a fixed point at which we declare: 'This is who I am.' Life is fluid, ever-changing, and full of surprises, and maintaining a flexible self-concept can help us weather the inevitable storms of life. It's a commonly known engineering principle that rigidity leaves buildings vulnerable, unable to withstand the shaking movements of the ground during earthquakes. And psychologically we are built in a similar way. Holding rigid ideas about who we are makes us less able to cope with life's disruptions. Try, instead, to experience life as authentically as you can, while remaining connected to yourself and the people around you. This, in itself, is a powerful victory.

# CONCLUSION: HEALING IN PROGRESS

As you arrive at this final chapter, I hope that the words that have come before have helped you access a more aware, hopeful, and peaceful part of yourself. Being raised by emotionally immature parents means you were denied the safety and opportunity to be yourself as a child, and to develop into yourself as an adult. Many people with such experiences never find a way to look at themselves, their parents, and their childhoods honestly, or do the work needed to fill the emotional gaps they've been left with. But you have found the courage to heal. The courage to disrupt the emotional sediment that has been lying at the bottom of the water, so that you can clear some of it away and let the rest of it settle a bit differently. What a brave thing to do. It is also one of the most life-affirming actions you can take: to follow that part of you that says, 'Life can be better and I deserve a greater experience of life than my childhood set me up for.' It is the greatest testament to your drive for living well and fully.

## ARE WE THERE YET?

As part of my counseling training, I had to attend therapy (for the first time). I was completely unaware of how much work there was to do on myself, and had even less of an idea where to start. My therapist asked me what my goals were for the sessions. I was stumped and tried my best to think of how I might know when I felt better. Eventually I said, 'I want to be able to feel it when birds sing. I want to notice nature and enjoy what's around me.' (No small task for our planned six sessions!) On reflection, I think I was trying to say that I wanted to feel more alive. I wanted to feel less numb and I knew that there was beauty and joy out there that I couldn't access, because my thoughts were so loud and life felt like a survival mission. A few years later, I vividly remember sitting at my in-laws' house in the English countryside, completely still, listening to the wood pigeons and smelling spring, and feeling warm, content, alive, and unbothered by my thoughts. I'd made it (to that healing goal).

As I write this, I am 40 years old, with 15 years of therapeutic practice under my belt and around two decades of personal healing – and honestly, I am not sure there is a finish line when it comes to healing after childhood trauma. There are, however, many ways in which life can feel much, much better, brighter, and sharper. And many moments that lie ahead of you in which the time spent reflecting, processing, grieving, and making different choices will make your life feel more like yours.

## RECOGNIZING YOUR GROWTH

As we near the end of the book, let's take a moment to reflect on what your personal healing milestones, or quiet signs of progress, might be. So that when those moments arrive in the future, you'll be able to recognize them and honor how far you've come.

- What are some of your personal markers for progress as you heal?
- What do you hope will become different the more you heal?
- What changes can you look out for in yourself as signs that you are healing?

The biggest shifts in healing are often silent and barely noticeable to other people. Small moments when you quietly notice yourself feeling calmer, clearer, excited, or more content; or aware of the smell of flowers or the sound of the wood pigeon; or when you hear your child's words with more clarity or become more aware of your own body. These small moments, that no one else would even notice, are some of the biggest wins. Healing is rarely a string of wins and triumphs, though. When I notice myself restarting old habits, or falling back into patterns that I thought were long-resolved, I try to remind myself of the nature of change, and the reality of healing.

The Cycle of Change Model is a useful guide for this. Developed by James Prochaska and Carlo DiClemente in the late 1970s and early 80s, it is a model that describes the stages people typically move through when making lasting behavioral or emotional changes.[1]

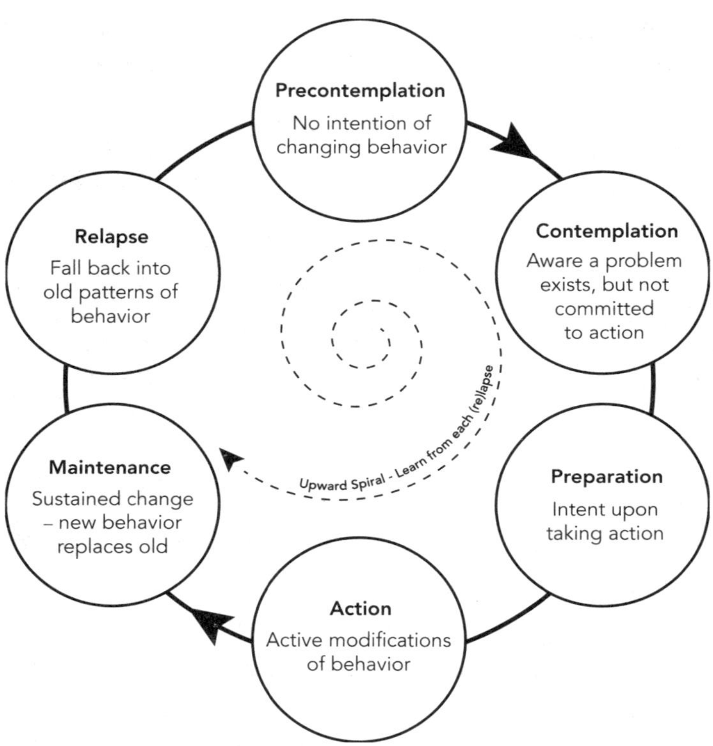


*The Cycle of Change Model*

It begins with **Precontemplation**, the stage of blissful (or not-so-blissful) unawareness before you realize the need for change. This is followed by **Contemplation**, in which you recognize a need for change but feel ambivalent. Next is **Preparation**, involving planning and small steps toward change, when you are living with an awareness of necessary shifts but have not yet gone all in.

Then comes the stage of **Action**, where active efforts are made to change behaviors or patterns. After that comes **Maintenance**, where the focus is on sustaining the new behavior and integrating it. We often move back and forth between the different stages, and sometimes, because we are human, we **Relapse** and fall back into old habits. The difference is that we then have an opportunity to learn and reenter the cycle with greater insight. Each relapse offers the chance of a deeper and more effective experience of the changing behavior. You can also exit the cycle of change for a particular behavior altogether, once you have integrated it enough for it to become part of how you are. The process of change is often nonlinear, and movement back and forth between stages is a natural part of growth.

Healing is ongoing because life is ongoing. Even if you dedicated 100 percent of your time to healing for a full year (which is impractical and not something I would recommend!), you will still experience something, at some point, that will make you feel like you're back at square one again. Because life happens in ways we can't control: parents pass away, divorce happens, illness comes from nowhere, perimenopause shows up, children grow up and leave, redundancies happen. Major life events can trigger old issues that we thought were long gone. They can also bring new and deeper versions of healing when we find ways to process and grieve them, and reaffirm our self-parenting skills as a result.

Each time you get curious with yourself about how you're feeling, or why you've been reacting in a certain way in your relationships, or consider why certain parts of life are feeling hard for you, you are finding more ways to enjoy life by releasing hidden layers of anxiety, self-doubt, sadness, and heavy mood. You are armoring yourself, becoming more emotionally sturdy, and giving yourself a better chance of recovering when life knocks you sideways. By staying gently in the loop of healing you are, effectively, turning your childhood wounds into a scar, and one thing that's certain is that it's much easier to live life with a scar than a wound. Healing doesn't need to be complete for you to start living. Healing *is* living. You are built to evolve and grow and regenerate. Living and healing go hand in hand; one can't fully happen without the other.

## YOU ARE THE KEY

I hope that by reading this book you have been able to release some of the pain you've been carrying from your past and make more sense of your relationship with your parents, and in doing so, move further toward a more authentic version of yourself. You have survived so much, and while I know that you are deeply resilient, I hope for a future for you that doesn't require you to be quite so strong. I hope that just because you can cope, it doesn't mean that you have to. But remember that you *always* have the capacity to bring yourself back: to recenter, to grieve and process, to embrace the good and the bad. To be strong and gentle at the same time. All of this lies within you. And as you keep finding new layers of peace and continue to discard old beliefs, stories, and versions of yourself, I'd love you to remember that you don't just hold the key to a more alive, enjoyable, and emotionally healthy life, *you are the key.* Your core self, inner resources, creativity, insight, and personal power are endless. Here's to a future filled with abundant life and fierce self-love.

# ENDNOTES


## Chapter 1: What Is Emotionally Immature Parenting?

1. Winnicott, D. W. (1960), 'The Theory of the Parent-Infant Relationship,' *International Journal of Psychoanalysis*, 41: 585–95.

## Chapter 2: You're Not Making a Fuss

1. Kumari, V. (2020), 'Emotional Abuse and Neglect: Time to Focus on Prevention and Mental Health Consequences,' *British Journal of Psychiatry*, 217(5): 597–99.

## Chapter 4: How Trauma Changes Us

1. Maté, G. with Maté, D. (2024), *The Myth of Normal: Illness, Health and Healing in a Toxic Culture*. London: Ebury Publishing.
2. Gilmore, J. H., *et al.* (2018), 'Imaging Structural and Functional Brain Development in Early Childhood,' *Nature Reviews Neuroscience*, 19(3): 123–37.
3. Teicher, M. H. and Samson, J. A. (2016), 'Enduring Neurobiological Effects of Childhood Abuse and Neglect,' *Journal of Child Psychology and Psychiatry*, 57(3): 241–66.
4. Kuzminskaite, E., *et al.* (2021), 'Childhood Trauma in Adult Depressive and Anxiety Disorders: An Integrated Review on Psychological and Biological Mechanisms in the NESDA Cohort,' *Journal of Affective Disorders*, 283: 179–91.
5. Helm, C., *et al.* (2008), 'The Link Between Childhood Trauma and Depression: Insights from HPA Axis Studies in Humans,' *Psychoneuroendocrinology*, 33(6): 693–710.
6. Wolff, M. S., *et al.* (2005), 'Exposures Among Pregnant Women Near the World Trade Center Site on 11 September 2001,' *Environmental Health Perspectives*, 113(6): 739–48.

7. Coussons-Read, M. (2013), 'Effects of Prenatal Stress on Pregnancy and Human Development: Mechanisms and Pathways,' *Obstetric Medicine*, 6(2): 52–7.

8. Smeeth, D., *et al.* (2021), 'The Role of Epigenetics in Psychological Resilience,' *The Lancet Psychiatry*, 8(7): 620–29.

9. Leuner, B. and Gould, E. (2010), 'Structural Plasticity and Hippocampal Function,' *Annual Review of Psychology*, 61: 111–C3.

10. Invigo, S. (2024), 'Overcoming Childhood Trauma: Understanding the Impact of Neuroplasticity and EMDR Therapy': thecenterfornewpathways.com/overcoming-childhood-trauma-understanding-the-impact-of-neuroplasticity-and-emdr-therapy/ [Accessed 26 July 2025].

11. Cremaldi, J. C. and Bhushan, B. (2018), 'Bioinspired Self-healing Materials: Lessons from Nature,' *Beilstein Journal of Nanotechnology*, 9: 907–35.

### Chapter 5: The Healing Power of Seeing Your Parents as People

1. Jung, C. G. (1969), 'A Study in the Process of Individuation,' in *The Collected Works of C. G. Jung, Volume 9-I*. Princeton, NJ: Princeton University Press, pp.290–354.

### Chapter 6: Accepting and Grieving the Hand You Were Dealt

1. de Bellefonds, C. (2021), 'When Your Baby Can Hear in the Womb': https://www.whattoexpect.com/pregnancy/fetal-development/fetal-hearing/ [Accessed 26 July 2025].

2. Frey, W. H. (1985), *Crying: The Mystery of Tears*. Minneapolis, MN: Winston Press.

3. Frey, W. H., *et al.* (1981), 'Effect of Stimulus on the Chemical Composition of Human Tears,' *American Journal of Ophthalmology*, 92(4): 559–67.

4. Schweizer, T. H., *et al.* (2017), 'Developmental Origins of Rumination in Middle Childhood: The Roles of Early Temperament and Positive Parenting,' *Journal of Clinical Child & Adolescent Psychology*, 47(SUP1): S409–S420.

### Chapter 7: You Make Sense

1. Maté, G. with Maté, D. (2024), *The Myth of Normal: Illness, Health and Healing in a Toxic Culture*. London: Ebury Publishing.

2. Brown, B. (2018), *The Gifts of Imperfection: Let Go of Who You Think You're Supposed to Be and Embrace Who You Are*. Center City, MN: Hazelden Publishing.

3. Rorty, A. O. (1980), *Explaining Emotions*. Oakland, CA: University of California Press.

4. Thümmler, R., *et al.* (2022), 'Strengthening Emotional Development and Emotion Regulation in Childhood – As a Key Task in Early Childhood Education,' *International Journal of Environmental Research and Public Health*, 19(7): 3978.

5. Taylor, J. B. (2009), *My Stroke of Insight*. New York, NY: New American Library.

## Chapter 8: Becoming Your Own Emotionally Mature Parent

1. https://psychologydictionary.org/internalization [Accessed 26 July 2025].

2. https://www.oxfordlearnersdictionaries.com/definition/english/nurture_1 [Accessed 26 July 2025].

3. Harlow, H. F., *et al.* (1965), 'Total Social Isolation in Monkeys,' *Proceedings of the National Academy of Sciences of the United States of America*, 54(1): 90–7.

4. Ekman, P. (1992), 'An Argument for Basic Emotions,' *Cognition and Emotion*, 6(3–4): 169–200.

5. Leisman, G. and Melillo, R. (2011), 'Infant and Childhood Frontal Lobe Development: Asymmetry and the Regulation of Temperament and Affect,' in *Frontal Lobe: Anatomy, Functions and Injuries*. Hauppauge, NY: Nova Scientific, pp.23–56.

## Chapter 9: Peace and Safety

1. Kenwood, M. M., *et al.* (2022), 'The Prefrontal Cortex, Pathological Anxiety, and Anxiety Disorders,' *Neuropsychopharmacology*, 47: 260–75.

2. Uytun, M. C. (2018), 'Development Period of Prefrontal Cortex' in *Prefrontal Cortex.* London: IntechOpen.

3. Bornstein, M. H. and Esposito, G. (2023), 'Coregulation: A Multilevel Approach via Biology and Behavior,' *Children*, 10(8): 1323.

4. Brown, B. (2015), *Daring Greatly: How the Courage to Be Vulnerable Transforms the Way We Live, Love, Parent, and Lead.* London: Penguin Life.

5. Northrup, K. (2019), *Do Less: A Revolutionary Approach to Time and Energy Management for Ambitious Women*. London: Hay House.

6. Dunckley, V. (2012), 'Electronic Screen Syndrome: An Unrecognized Disorder': www.psychologytoday.com/us/blog/mental-wealth/201207/electronic-screen-syndrome-an-unrecognized-disorder [Accessed 26 July 2025].

7. Ehrlich, P. R. (2024), *Humanity's Group Size Problem*. New Haven, CT: Yale University Press.

8. Paraschiv, P. (2025), 'The Influences of Physical Exercises on the Nervous System,' *Bulletin of the Polytechnic Institute of Iași*, 70(3):21–5.

9. Franco, L. S., *et al.* (2017), 'A Review of the Benefits of Nature Experiences: More Than Meets the Eye,' *International Journal of Environmental Research and Public Health*, 14: 864.

10. Sutton-Smith, B. (1999), *The Ambiguity of Play*. Cambridge, MA: Harvard University Press.

11. Lubbers, K., *et al.* (2023), 'Adult Play and Playfulness: A Qualitative Exploration of its Meanings and Importance,' *The Journal of Play in Adulthood*, 5(2): 1–19.

## Chapter 10: Learning to Love in Peace

1. Brown, B. (2015), *Daring Greatly: How the Courage to Be Vulnerable Transforms the Way We Live, Love, Parent, and Lead*. London: Penguin Books.

2. Mikulincer, M. and Shaver, P. R. (2017), *Attachment in Adulthood: Structure, Dynamics, and Change*. New York City, NY: Guilford Publications.

3. Dansby Olufowote, R. A., *et al.* (2020), 'How Can I Become More Secure?: A Grounded Theory of Earning Secure Attachment,' *Journal of Marital and Family Therapy*, 46(3): 489–506.

4. Saunders, R., *et al.* (2011), 'Pathways to Earned-security: The Role of Alternative Support Figures,' *Attachment & Human Development*, 13(4): 403–20.

5. Ward, K. (n.d.), 'Rupture and Repair: Responding to Disrespect': https://parentingplace.nz/resources/getting-back-on-track-after-everyday-upsets [Accessed 26 July 2025].

6. Premack, D., and Woodruff, G. (1978), 'Does the Chimpanzee Have a Theory of Mind?', *Behavioral and Brain Sciences*, 1(4): 515–26.

## Chapter 11: Who Am I Now?

1. Beck, J. S. (2020), *Cognitive Behavior Therapy: Basics and Beyond*. New York City, NY: Guilford Publications.

2. Rogers, C. (1977), *On Becoming a Person: A Therapist's View of Psychotherapy*. London: Constable.

3. Watts, A. (1966), 'Mysticism and Morality': https://www.organism.earth/library/document/mysticism-and-morality [Accessed 26 July 2025].

## Conclusion: Healing in Progress

1. Prochaska, J. O. and DiClemente, C. C. (1983), 'Stages and Processes of Self-change of Smoking: Toward an Integrative Model of Change,' *Journal of Consulting and Clinical Psychology*, 51(3): 39–95.

# RESOURCES

## BOOKS

Here are some recommendations for further reading:

- Dr. Nadine Burke Harris, *Toxic Childhood Stress: The Legacy of Early Trauma and How to Heal*, Bluebird, 2020
- Bessel van der Kolk, *The Body Keeps the Score: Brain, Mind, and Body in the Healing of Trauma*, Penguin Books, 2015
- Dr. Amir Levine and Rachel Heller, M.A., *Attached: Are You Anxious, Avoidant or Secure?*, Pan Macmillan, 2019
- Gabor Maté, *When the Body Says No: The Cost of Hidden Stress*, Ebury Publishing, 2019
- Gabor Maté and Daniel Maté, *The Myth of Normal: Illness, Health and Healing in a Toxic Culture*, Ebury Publishing, 2024
- Dr. Karyl McBride, *Will I Ever Be Good Enough?: Healing the Daughters of Narcissistic Mothers*, Atria Books, 2023
- Kelly McDaniel, *Mother Hunger: How Adult Daughters Can Understand and Heal from Lost Nurturance, Protection and Guidance*, Hay House, 2021

- Philippa Perry, *The Book You Wish Your Parents Had Read (and Your Children Will Be Glad That You Did)*, Penguin Books, 2020
- Margot Sunderland, *What Every Parent Needs To Know: A Psychologist's Guide to Raising Happy, Nurtured Children*, Dorling Kindersley, 2023
- Mark Wolynn, *It Didn't Start with You: How Inherited Family Trauma Shapes Who We Are and How to End the Cycle*, Ebury Publishing, 2022

## ORGANIZATIONS

Below, you'll find details of well-being support organizations in your home country.

### Australia

- **Beyond Blue** supports Australians experiencing anxiety, depression, and related issues through specialized programs. The website has helpline numbers. www.beyondblue.org.au
- **The Mental Health Foundation Australia** offers a range of services, including counseling, support groups, and educational programs aimed at promoting mental health and providing assistance to individuals facing mental health challenges. www.mhfa.org.au
- **Lifeline**: 13 11 14 (24 hours). Crisis support and suicide prevention helpline.
- **SANE Australia**: 1800 187 263 (10 a.m.–8 p.m. Mon–Fri). National mental health organization for people with recurring, persistent, or complex mental health issues and trauma, and for their families, friends, and communities. www.sane.org

## Canada

- **Canadian Mental Health Association (CMHA)**: 9-8-8 (24 hours). One of Canada's oldest and largest community mental health organizations, working nationwide to promote mental health, prevent mental illness, and support recovery. Call or text for support in English or French. www.cmha.ca
- **Mood Disorders Society of Canada (MDSC):** (613) 921-5565. Helps adults and families affected by depression, bipolar disorder, anxiety, PTSD, and other mood disorders through peer support networks, national community programs, and online resources. www.mdsc.ca

## India

- **AASRA**: 22-2754-6669 (24 hours). Free confidential helpline in Hindi and English. The website lists other services across India. www.aasra.info
- **Mental Health Mission India**: 88-9933-3777. MHM provides free counseling via phone or email, along with community wellness workshops in schools, workplaces, and communities. www.mhmindia.org

## New Zealand

- **Mental Health Foundation of New Zealand**: call or text 1737 (24 hours). Charity dedicated to promoting positive mental health and well-being, advocating for mental health awareness, and providing resources and support to individuals and communities. www.mentalhealth.org.nz
- **Lifeline**: 0800 543 354 (0800 LIFELINE) or free text 4357 (HELP); 24 hours.

## South Africa

- **South African Depression and Anxiety Group (SADAG)**: 0800 567 567 (24 hours). The country's largest mental health organization offers counseling services, support groups, and a referral call center. www.sadag.org
- **LifeLine Johannesburg**: 0861 322 322. Provides free mental health services, including telephone, face-to-face, and online counseling appointments. www.lifelinejhb.org.za

## United Kingdom

- **SANEline helpline**: 0300 304 7000 (4 p.m.–10 p.m. every day). A national out-of-hours helpline offering specialist emotional support to anyone affected by mental illness.
- **Mind**: 0300 123 3393 (9 a.m.–6 p.m. Mon–Fri). Mind provides advice, information, counseling, and support to people experiencing mental health problems. www.mind.org.uk
- **Samaritans**: 116 123 (24 hours). Crisis support and suicide prevention helpline. www.samaritans.org
- Find an accredited therapist via the following websites: www.psychotherapy.org.uk or www.babcp.com

## United States

- **Mental Health America**: 988 (calls or text). National nonprofit dedicated to the promotion of mental health, well-being, and condition prevention. www.mhanational.org
- **National Alliance on Mental Illness (NAMI)**: 1-800-950-6264 (10 a.m.–10 p.m. E.T. Mon–Fri); text NAMI to 62640. NAMI offers advocacy and workshops, and has local affiliates in all 50 states. www.nami.org

# ACKNOWLEDGMENTS

Thank you, firstly, to Hay House, and in particular to Kezia Bayard-White. When you contacted me after finding and trawling through my thoughts on Instagram, I started to believe that maybe that manifestation stuff I'd heard about might be real after all! Sitting in our first meeting with the Hay House team continues to be one of my most surreal and affirming experiences. To see you all so enthused about a book about emotionally immature parenting was incredible, and to have such an amazing group of women who all 'got it' and who had faith in me to be the one to do this topic justice was amazing. From the start of this process it has felt as though this book was destined to be written. I now realize that it was actually being created in the back of my mind for years, and being in such safe, supportive hands with Hay House meant I could bring it to the forefront with ease.

Thank you to my lovely husband, Tom, who has supported me throughout with encouraging words, chapter read-throughs, and trips to the park with the children when deadlines were looming. I can't wait to do the same for you one day when your publisher finds you. Thank you for continuing to be my encouraging and steady port, whenever life feels stormy. And to the lovely Crossley family, who have seen me through the transition from 'girl on Tom's university course,' to in-law, to psychotherapist, and now to author. I'm so grateful for your ongoing interest in my career and the book.

To my mum: thank you for all the effort you put into family life, and for doing your absolute best in raising us. I'm aware that the work I do and the topic of this book have been difficult for you to understand, but I hope in time you come to see it as something important, necessary, and valuable for those who need it. To Nan: you've not been fully able to witness the writing of this book, but the many years of your unconditional love and constant belief that I could do anything that I put my mind to has been with me throughout.

To my friends, who never tired of asking me how writing was going – even when we were on the other side of the world to each other – and who patiently listened as I waffled on about chapter titles and word counts. Thank you to Naomi, my constant cheerleader. You've been more excited for me than I've been for myself at times, and your words of encouragement during our weekly 'Wednesday waffle' video calls helped bring this book to life. To lovely Rebecca: our chats about childhood and motherhood – and our shared determination to give ourselves more than we were given – not only bring me huge comfort, but threads of those conversations are woven throughout these pages. And to Karen, for believing in my potential long before Break the Cycle Coaching existed, or a book deal was on the cards. Your 'hype girl' energy (historically delivered over midweek cocktails, and more recently in hurried voice notes in between naps and nappy changes) has been a huge boost in times of self-doubt.

And finally, thank you to everyone who has ever walked into my therapy room or taken one of my courses, ready and willing to think about the hard stuff that we all do our best to avoid. Your bravery, trust, and honesty have given this book its heartbeat.

Gabrielle McMillan

# ABOUT THE AUTHOR

**Sian Morgan-Crossley** is a London-born psychotherapist working in psychodynamic counseling and CBT. She spent 10 years working in the NHS, helping those with depression and anxiety, and built a bustling private practice. After becoming a mother, she decided to venture into the world of online business and Break the Cycle Coaching was born in 2020. Since then, she has helped thousands of people across the world with her online courses and membership community, which are focused on different aspects of healing after childhood trauma. She also trains other therapists and coaches in working with people on their mother wound, and hosts *The Healing in Progress Podcast*. Sian's hope is that her work reaches and helps those whose childhood didn't give them the skills or self-worth needed to thrive and enjoy adulthood.

**breakthecyclecoaching.co.uk**

**@breakthecycle_coaching**

**@siancrossley9027**

We hope you enjoyed this Hay House book. If you'd like to receive our online catalog featuring additional information on Hay House books and products, or if you'd like to find out more about the Hay Foundation, please contact:

Hay House LLC, P.O. Box 5100, Carlsbad, CA 92018-5100
(760) 431-7695 or (800) 654-5126
www.hayhouse.com® • www.hayfoundation.org

---

***Published in Australia by:***
Hay House Australia Publishing Pty Ltd
18/36 Ralph St., Alexandria NSW 2015
*Phone:* +61 (02) 9669 4299
www.hayhouse.com.au

***Published in the United Kingdom by:***
Hay House UK Ltd
1st Floor, Crawford Corner,
91–93 Baker Street, London W1U 6QQ
*Phone:* +44 (0)20 3927 7290
www.hayhouse.co.uk

***Published in India by:***
Hay House Publishers (India) Pvt Ltd
Muskaan Complex, Plot No. 3,
B-2, Vasant Kunj, New Delhi 110 070
*Phone:* +91 11 41761620
www.hayhouse.co.in

---